Understanding Social Media for Business

I0477326

A Simple Simon's Guide

Edition 1.02 -2016
First Published March 2016
Simple Simons Publishing

How and Why to Use Social Media
in Your Business Today
An absolute **MUST** read for anyone
who needs to know more about Growing their
business using Social Media

A FREE Gift for You

Thank you very much for purchasing this book

As a thank you, I would like to offer you a gift

which can be downloaded from our website

www.SimpleSimonsPublishing.com/freegift

Copyright Notice 2015

Table of Contents

Forward

Having a keen interest in technology, I like to keep abreast of the latest developments. However, the biggest problem is information overload.

With the whole world being connected where the answer to everything is at our fingertips, it is difficult to filter out the relevant information. It was not that long ago when the must-have business and personal management tool was the Filofax.

These days, there are thousands of to-do list and business management programs available. They profess to simplify the process of running your life and business. However simply finding the one that suits you can take weeks.

Time is becoming more precious and instead of making our life easier, the demand on our time has increased. Therefore it is important that we filter out the noise, and reduce the content that we allow into our lives. Simple Simon Guides do exactly that.

This is the reason we created the Simple Simon series. We are the noise cancelling system for your life.

The idea is to take, what can be an over-complicated explanation, and boil it down to its essence. In other words, to simplify it into digestible, bite-size chunks, that will allow the reader to understand the important aspects of the topic without going into too much technical detail.

More information can be found at
www.simplesimonspublishing.com

Who is Simple Simon?

Don't be fooled into thinking he is a fool; Simple Simon is a smart guy. He is usually busy, works hard, and doesn't like to waste his time.

He wants and needs to be informed, but is not looking for long-winded, step-by-step tutorials, but more of a synopsis or summary of a topic or particular subject.

He likes to keep things simple where he can and doesn't require an in-depth understanding of the topic in question.

Preferably, he wants and needs to know enough to be able to discuss these subjects in an intelligent way with his team, business partners, and colleagues.

As an example, such topics could include the following:

- "I know everyone is on Facebook but isn't it just for kids and funny cat pictures?"
- "I understand the benefits of advertising on the internet, without having to know how to setup Adwords on Google. What I need to know is what other options are out there?"
- "I don't want to know how to install and set up Wordpress. But I would like to know why I should use this in my business, as opposed to an HTML template?"

Understanding Social Media is the first in the 'Simple Simon' series and provides the reader with an overview of some of the social network sites available today and how to use them in your business.

1. Introduction

It's hard to imagine the world without social media. Sites like Facebook and Twitter have totally changed the way we communicate and share information with each other. There's one thing for sure: social media is here to stay.

As a business owner, social media is something you simply can't afford to ignore. It can help you seek out new customers and build stronger relationships with existing ones. Furthermore, it enables you to connect more easily with other individuals and organisations that can help you grow your business.

You can use social media to spot new opportunities and trends within your industry. It allows you to get feedback on new product ideas, and see what the competition is up to. You can use it as a tool to improve customer service, increase brand loyalty, and so much more. The possibilities are virtually endless.

If you're reading this book, then you might already recognise the huge opportunity with which social media provides you. However, maybe you're not sure exactly how to exploit the opportunities. As with anything, it will only truly generate results for your business, if it is implemented and managed the right way.

This is not to say that social media is complicated. Or, that it has to take up large amounts of time, effort, and money, to be effective. What it *does* mean is you need to know *what* you're doing and *why* you're doing it. Subsequently, be able to implement your strategy on a consistent, ongoing basis. This book should help you in that regard.

Some of you might also feel a little skeptical about social media, and need a little convincing why it's going to be good for your business. You might feel concerned that it isn't the best use of your energy and resources. Also, you might be worried that social media could do more harm than good.

This book should hopefully provide you with a realistic look at what this platform can do for your business. Additionally, it will address some of those issues by showing you practical ways of putting it all into action.

Essentially, this book will show why you should be using social media and how to use it - *the right way.*

This book is for the smart business owner who wants to get an overview, or 'bird's- eye view' of social media. Furthermore, to understand why he or she should be using it, and how to use it effectively. It is designed to be both practical and realistic, with an emphasis on helping you to achieve real world results.

What You'll Get Out of This Book

By the time you've finished reading, you should have a good understanding of:

- What social media is – and where it's heading.
- How it can be beneficial to your business.
- The main social media platforms, who uses them, and the various advantages and disadvantages of each site.
- Effective strategies you can implement to get substantial results.
- Common mistakes businesses make—and how to avoid making them.

Before we begin, I just want to mention a couple of things . . .

While using social networking sites can provide great benefits to your business; it's important to understand it isn't a magic pill. To see tangible results, you'll need to have a clear strategy and then implement that strategy on a consistent basis. If you can do that, then you should be very pleased by what social media can help you achieve.

Go through the book, take plenty of notes and then implement what you learn. The best plan is to formulate your social media strategy (we cover that later in the book) then just take action. The quicker you do so, the quicker you'll start seeing results. You'll most likely make plenty of mistakes along the way, but that's certainly not a bad thing.

Social Media does have a learning curve. However, it isn't as scary as some people believe, and over time you'll become more confident using it. One of the great things about this methodology is the fact that you can try things and say, "Wow, that worked great!" Or, "Blimey, that didn't work like we thought it would. Let's do this instead." The Internet makes it super easy to try ideas and see the results they bring, without investing too much time and effort.

Ready to begin?

Let's get into it!

~Simple Simon

2. Introduction to Social Media

What is Social Media?

Before we go any further, it's worth defining what social media is:

> Social Media:
> *Virtual communities and networks*
> *that allow people to communicate*
> *and share information with one*
> *another through the internet. Social*
> *Media platforms are usually accessed*
> *via computers, mobile phones, or*
> *tablets.*

You might not realise it, but social media has been around since the 1990s. However, things have changed significantly over the years. There were a number of forums and newsgroups set up where people exchanged views, information, and ideas with each other.

One of the first social networking websites was GeoCities that was established in the mid-90s. It allowed users to create their own websites and then assign the pages they had created to build virtual *cities*.

GeoCities was at one time, the third most visited website on the Internet. However, the website that arguably kick-started this phenomenon was MySpace, which launched in 2003.

MySpace allowed users to post their profile, add friends as contacts and share information such as messages and photos with others. It served to bring people together, and it was a massive success. That was until the launch of the site that effectively killed off MySpace as a mainstream social networking website: Facebook.

While Facebook is still the largest social networking website, people also tend to think of sites such as Twitter, YouTube, Google+, Linkedin, Instagram, and Pinterest. These sites have also become a daily part of our lives.

Each of these channels functions in a different way and have a different focus. However, each one is ultimately about keeping in contact and sharing things with others. Therefore, allowing various people to interact with you and your company.

Social Interaction - Self-Hosted and Hosted Solutions

Most companies use one of the more popular hosted social media sites (such as Facebook and the other sites we are going to cover in this book). However it is worth noting, there are also self-hosted options that allow companies to run their own social. Software like Elgg (self-hosted) or Ning (hosted) allows you to have complete control over the way your social media site looks and feels, as well as how people interact with you.

The downside to this, is you have to generate all of the buzz to get visitors to your website. Whereas the popular social media sites already have a massive amount of traffic coming to them. You can then funnel that traffic to your pages using a variety of free and paid methods. It is much easier to get 10,000 visitors to your Facebook profile, for example, than it would be to your self-hosted social network.

The benefit of solutions like Elgg and Ning, is you have 100% control of every aspect of the site. This is unlike any of the other third party options, which have rules and regulations that you cannot influence. Some sites like Facebook, for example, often change the layout and the way they work, much to the annoyance of its users.

Who Uses Social Media?

Social Media usage is certainly widespread—and the increased numbers of people using it over the last few years are staggering.

According to 2014 research, some 73% of online adults use social media. When you break down the figures further, approximately 71% use Facebook and 42% are using multiple social networks. To put some figures next to those percentages, Statista says there were 1.61 billion social media users in 2013. That figure is expected to reach a whopping 2.33 billion users by 2017.

I'm sure you'll agree that is a heck of a lot of people – and it's likely that figure is only going to grow and grow. When you consider less than a billion people were using social media as recently as 2010, then it certainly puts things into perspective.

In addition, it's worth noting that all age groups use social media, albeit to varying degrees. 2014 statistics show the biggest users of these websites, are unsurprisingly 18 to 29-year-olds. And, 89% of that demographic are using social networking sites. At the other end of the age spectrum, and a slightly more surprising statistic - 49% of people aged 65+ use social networking sites. That is certainly a significant number of people.

So which social networks are people using?

Facebook currently leads the pack with 1.28 billion users in June 2014. The Chinese social network Qzone is in second place with 644 million users. Google+ comes in third with 343 million users.

Linkedin, Twitter, and Tumblr closely follow with 300, 255 and 230 million users respectively.

Social Media and Business

While social media began as a way for individuals to communicate and share content, it now incorporates almost every type of business or organisation imaginable. Businesses around the globe use it to find new customers and build relationships with existing ones. They range from individual entrepreneurs, through to internationally recognised brands. Virtually every type of business can benefit from using this medium.

Although it can certainly be an excellent business tool (if used in the right way), it's also something of which many businesses use "because everyone else uses it." However, such entities don't understand exactly *why* they should be using it, *what* it can do for their business, or *how* to use it properly. This leads to businesses wasting huge amounts of time, money and effort—and approaching social media in the *wrong* way.

Simon Says: "It is essential to be clear on exactly what you want to achieve through social media, then devise a comprehensible strategy."

In practice, almost all businesses should be using it to some degree. Given the types of statistics we have just mentioned, it's something that just cannot be ignored. Furthermore, those who do are certainly missing out on a huge opportunity.

In addition, it's worth emphasising the point that social media can be of huge benefit to businesses of all sizes. It's a common misconception that it's only large multinational brands with huge marketing budgets that can benefit by using these channels. The reality is quite different. Even the smallest business can reap the

—

rewards, without having to spend large amounts of time and money on managing their campaigns.

Different Businesses Should Use Social Media in Different Ways

Every business should be using social media, but the way in which they use it will greatly vary. It depends on the type of business they are, the industry in which they're operating, and the market they are targeting.

Take, for example, a designer fashion retailer who targets people in the 20 to 40 age category. Compare that fashion retailer to a company that manufactures and sells large-button mobile phones. Those phones that are aimed at older people who have poor eyesight and struggle with using regular phones. Both of these companies should be using social media—but the way in which they would use it is quite different.

Let's first look at the fashion retailer. A large proportion of their target audience is likely to be big users of the various networks. Therefore, there is a fantastic opportunity to use this platform to market directly to these people.

They could, for example, use Facebook as a way of directly selling their products by using an app such as Shopify. This app turns their Facebook page into an online ecommerce store. In addition, they could use Facebook and Twitter to keep their customers updated with the latest fashion lines, news and developments.

They could post photos of the latest stock ("look what's just arrived!") and share details of coupon codes with their social media followers. Their followers can then use these codes to gain exclusive discounts off products in their online store.

Now let's take a look at the large button phone company. At first thought, you might wonder why such a business would want to use social media. Surely their target audience won't be using sites like Facebook and Twitter, would they?

This is probably true, however, the company could get results by marketing to the family, friends, and careers of its end users. These are people whom most likely *will* be active on Facebook and Twitter. They could use social media to raise awareness about their products. In turn, they could provide the peace of mind knowing that elderly people will be able to contact them more easily.
A good example would be in an emergency.

However, this company might concentrate the majority of its networking efforts by connecting with other companies. These other companies might be able to help spread the message about the former's products. For example, they could use Linkedin to network with opticians. These opticians may be willing to suggest the product to elderly customers, or anyone else who may otherwise struggle to use a normal phone.

These are of course just two examples, as there are hundreds of different ways to use social media. The point is, you should be totally clear on *why* you are using it, to *whom* you are targeting, and *what* result are you aiming toward. It would be easy for the phone company to just throw up a Facebook page, post information about their products, and leave it at that.

You may very well decide to concentrate your efforts on just one or two social networking platforms. It depends on what your customers are using. Let's say for example you've done research and identified your customers are heavy Twitter users but don't use Google+. You might then decide to concentrate the majority of your efforts on Twitter. Of course the opposite might be true, as it's all about knowing how your specific target market uses which network.

Simon Says: "Concentrate on the social media sites that your audience spends the most time using."

As a business owner, you need to learn to do your research, think for yourself, and not always follow the pack.

What Can Social Media Do for Your Business?

We will delve into this in more detail later on, but let's quickly cover some of the most obvious benefits when using social media:

- **It can help you find new customers** – for example, by using Facebook advertising to attract people to your fan page and website.

- **It enables you to build a relationship with your customers** – for example, by using Facebook to share content that people in your target market will find useful.

- **It can help you to improve customer service** – for example, by using Twitter to answer customer queries quickly, and point people in the direction where they can get more information.

- **It builds trust with your customers** – because social media is transparent and people can see issues or problems with your products and services. And, they'll notice how well you deal with them.

  It helps you listen to what your customers are saying, and what they want – so you can tweak your products or services to better suit your customers' needs.

In a nutshell, social media can help you find new customers, and it can help you turn those customers into *repeat* customers. What I call *raving fans*. Of course, it's also worth bearing in mind that these sites are only effective if they're used in the right way.

These various networks can provide an opportunity for businesses to spread positive messages about their brand. However, they can just as easily be used to share customers' negative experiences. Smart businesses can use social media to turn these negative experiences into positive ones. However, if that fails, or if the business deals with the issue inappropriately, the results can be disastrous.

You also have to consider this type of medium needs to be used responsibly. You can, for example, use a site such as Twitter or Facebook to share content your audience might find useful. However, if that content is misjudged, or if it's posted too often, it can easily start to annoy the very people whom it should be engaging.

How Do Businesses Use Social Media?

Almost every type of organisation you can imagine uses social media, from solo entrepreneurs right through to some of the largest brands in the world. The way that they use social media varies greatly of course – some will have a presence on just some of the social networks, while others will seemingly be everywhere.

Different businesses also have different goals of what they hope to gain from using social media. Understanding why you are there in the first place is definitely half the battle when it comes to using it successfully.

Summary Points

- **Social Media Definition:** Virtual communities and networks that allow people to communicate and share information with one another through the internet. Social Media platforms are usually accessed via computers, mobile phones or tablets, either by using a web browser or software application.

- Social Media usage is widespread, with some 73% of online adults using it.

- Social Media can be used in many different ways. No two businesses should have the same strategy for using social media as it depends on factors such as the nature of the business, objectives and target audience.

- Using social media has many different benefits. It can help businesses to find new customers, build relationships, improve customer service, and more.

3. Why Use Social Media?

We've already covered some of the things social media can do for your business. However, in this chapter, we're going to discuss its benefits in much more detail by using some specific examples.

Before we get into why you should be using social media, let's look at the various attitudes business owners take. Additionally, we'll examine some of the reasons why businesses *don't* use such methods.

Social Media Believers . . . to Social Media Sceptics

Business owners tend to have wildly different views and experiences when it comes to social media.

At one end of the scale, there are those who truly understand the value of using it, and are already harnessing its power to grow their business. They are prepared to think outside of the box. They understand the value of building campaigns and events that create a buzz.

They encourage their followers to get involved, to participate and share their content with their friends and colleagues. They are using social media every day and are excited by the results they're seeing.

In addition, there are also many people who understand its huge potential but aren't quite sure how to get the best out of it. Perhaps they have already set up their accounts, but feel like they're doing it all 'wrong.' However, they are keen to learn and believe, if given time, they'll achieve the results in which they are striving.

At the opposite end of the scale, there are the social media sceptics. People who fit into this group see this medium as a necessary evil and don't understand what all the fuss is about. While they have set up their accounts and make the occasional post, they don't see the value in running social media campaigns. However due to their lack of effort, are inevitably proved right.

They may view social media as an unproven avenue and perhaps they think it's an ineffective sales tool. They may be worried it doesn't provide them with a tangible return on investment. They may also feel their time and money would be better spent on other areas.

Another common viewpoint amongst sceptics is that it's not a business tool. They tend to think of it as somewhere people just share videos of cats doing silly things, or post embarrassing photos of themselves. Although this is a big reason people visit social networking sites, businesses are becoming an even bigger part of its social make-up.

You need to consider the *fun* nature these sites provide, with a golden opportunity to grab people's attention. Plus, this creates a conversation to draw them in as well. A good recent example of this was Air New Zealand. The airline used social media to share their latest Hobbit-themed in-flight safety video.

The video attracted Hobbit fans from all over the world and was released ahead of the final film in the Hobbit trilogy. It resulted in the video being shared hundreds of thousands of times on social media. Although it can be slightly trickier for smaller businesses to create results on that scale, it's certainly possible.

It also gives you an idea of how something that's fun and is also related to your business, can go viral globally. You can spread your message to a massive audience if you're engaging, creative, and provide value.

You most likely already know where you fit within the realm of social media viewpoints. Perhaps you can see why you can't afford to ignore this valuable platform. You know there are good things that can come out of using it. But at the same time, you're not sure what can realistically be achieved, or how to go about it.

In addition, you might have tried social media but felt disappointed with the results you achieved. You know it can have so much more impact, however, it just doesn't seem to be happening for you. On the other hand, maybe you are a sceptic? If that's you, then I hope I can change your opinion.

Why You Can't Afford to Ignore Social Media

Maybe you fall into the sceptics' camp? Or perhaps you know you should be more involved, but you don't have time, or don't know how to network? If that's the case, I have some bad news for you:

Social Media isn't going away, and its use is only going to grow. For many businesses this means, by ignoring social media, it will result in missing out on huge opportunities. Additionally, they'll be left behind by their competition. If you're not using it in your business, it's quite likely your competitors ARE.

They're stealing your customers and gaining a greater awareness of the market. In turn, this means they can conduct better marketing, improve their products and services, and effectively cater to people's needs. If you're a smart business owner, you really shouldn't be choosing to ignore its potential.

It's much better to start now, and as time goes on, you'll become more familiar with its benefits. You'll see what works for your specific business (and what doesn't). This includes the individual circumstances your company operates within.

Some Common Reasons Why Businesses Don't Use Social Media

Almost all businesses should be using it to some degree. However, many organisations fail to do so. Here are some common reasons I've heard businesses give, as to why they aren't using social media...

The Cost - *"We can't afford it."*

It's true, hiring a marketing specialist or social media agency to devise and implement your strategy, can be expensive. Furthermore, businesses may feel it's unrealistic to hire somebody to sit there all day and update Twitter, or post to Facebook. However the fact is, social media is a very cheap way to advertise compared to traditional methods.

As you put together your networking strategy and implement it consistently, it will have an upfront cost. Typically this pertains to the time involved. Therefore you should be looking at it as an *investment* in your business.

If you execute your strategy effectively, it should generate a good return on investment. As a result, it will pull back the costs involved with managing it many times over. In addition, it isn't always necessary to hire an expensive marketing agency to manage your accounts. Or as some people do, hire a dedicated social media specialist. There are several cheaper options you can consider to get started. The question is, "can you afford not to?"

The Time - *"We just don't have the time."*

Many businesses are extremely busy handling day-to-day operations. They simply may feel they don't have time to get involved. Although companies are under a great deal of pressure, marketing will always remain an <u>essential</u> ingredient in any successful business. I would argue social media as it is today, is one of the best tools you can have in your marketing arsenal.

It's important to emphasise that it's certainly necessary to be actively networking. However it needn't be time-consuming, nor should take all day. In fact, I would actively discourage spending too much time on it.

Once everything is up and running, it only requires spending a few minutes a day updating or posting to your various pages. You can even get automated software to do this task for you. Plus, you could outsource the task to a freelancer or social marketing agency.

Simon Says: "You can write your posts in bulk and use software to post automatically at the best time of day for your followers."

Understanding - *"I don't understand social media, plus it's too complicated."*

One of the most common issues businesses owners have with online networking, is they find it overwhelming. Even if you understand how it can help your business, it's easy to feel like it has too steep a learning curve. And, that it's not something that needs to be prioritised. You might feel confused with the different avenues within its parameters. Or, you may have heard conflicting advice from different experts.

It's certainly true there are a lot of different things to think about regarding social media. Yet it should be comforting to know, that it's relatively simple. That is, once you're clear on exactly what you want to get out of it, and how you're going to approach it.

Importance - "It's a waste of time."

Many business owners like to concentrate on strategies in which they feel will gain an instant result. For example, they have no problem having their sales team use the phone an entire morning, to contact different businesses and make appointments for the next week.

They can instantly measure their results, by tracking how many appointments are made vs. the number of companies that have been called.

On the other hand, they feel posting links to industry-related content on Twitter is somehow a waste of time. Instead, they want to have their Twitter feed post links to products which are available to buy on their website. Consequently, they are surprised when they achieve poor results.

Risk - "It's too risky."

I've heard CEOs describe social media as being *too risky*. Perhaps they're worried about the damage a negative comment concerning their company on Facebook could have on their business. Or, they may feel if they make a mistake on Twitter, it could do a great deal of harm to their brand.

Here's something to think about: People will be talking about your business on social media whether you're on it or not. In addition, if it's correctly managed, then it's possible to turn any negativity into a positive.

4. What Can Social Media Do for Your Business?

Now that we have looked at some of the attitudes businesses take toward social media, let's now turn our attention to what it can do for your business.

It Can Help You Find New Customers

One of the main benefits of social media is, it can help you find new customers and clients. You can use Facebook advertising, for example, to acquire new prospects, capture their details, and promote your products on a continuous basis.

It Can Help You Build Relationships with Your Customers

Another key reward from social networking is, it can help you build strong relationships with your customers. These platforms are places where people go to maintain contact with those whom they care about – and this certainly includes businesses. You can use it to communicate regularly with your customers, build engagement, and ultimately increase brand loyalty.

Note: Using social media to contact people, does **not** mean using it to promote *stuff* all of the time. In other words, it's not about trying to sell, sell and sell some more. But, if you use it in an ethical and correct manner, you'll bring value to your audience and direct them to things they'll find interesting.

It Builds Trust with Your Customers

By allowing open and transparent communication, social media enables prospective and existing customers to see any issues or problems that exist with your products or services. They can witness exactly how you deal with such occurrences. If it's approached in the correct way, it provides a fantastic opportunity to promote trust, and build confidence in your company and brand.

Let's say somebody tweets you on Twitter for example. They then tell you, how disappointed they felt in your customer service when they had a problem with one of your products. Your company replies back to the person, apologises for the problem, and offers to call the person to discuss the issue.

Later that day, the customer replies again to the initial tweet. He or she thanks Liz in customer service for her kind help and states the problem is now solved. Other people then see the exchange of tweets, and they're impressed by how the company dealt with the issue.

Remember, your customers understand products or services, sometimes have glitches. It's how they think you will deal with those accordingly that matters. That may, in fact, decide whether they choose to purchase from you or not. Social Media can be a wonderful tool for showing people you genuinely care about your customers. Moreover, you're prepared to go the extra mile to help them.

Simon Says: "Think carefully about how you respond to negative feedback on social media. By showing a sense of attentive customer service, you can turn a negative into a positive."

It Can Help You Improve Customer Service

This one follows on the previous point. Businesses of all sizes are increasingly using social media to improve customer service. Also, to provide an easy way for customers to contact them when they have a query or problem.

You can, for example, use a site such as Twitter to answer customer queries and point people in the direction for assistance. Not only does this provide a convenient way for people to get in touch, but it can also help minimise the number of people who are asking the same questions.

When you answer a question, you should also add it to your FAQ or customer service page. This is so next time if the same question arises, you can simply post the short answer and a link to the relevant page. You can also, over time, post questions from your FAQ or customer support pages with a link back to the page in question.

It will encourage people to start looking there, and hopefully spend more time on your website. This lessens the amount of time your staff spends answering common questions. Furthermore, it also provides the customer with a quicker way of finding their desired answer. Another common phenomenon is when your followers often answer negative feedback or comments on your behalf. By receiving this kind of support from others, it increases your reputation and credibility.

It Helps You Build Your Brand and Increases Awareness

One of the biggest challenges in marketing your business is standing out from your competitors. It's imperative for people to remember you. To do this, it's important to have a strong brand. Moreover, keeping that brand at the forefront in the minds of your audience. Social Media can help you to do that, and more.

You can, for example, post regular updates to your Facebook fan page. Not only does this reminds people that you exist, but it also builds your brand. In other words, demonstrating to people your company is an authority in the industry.

Imagine your business is real estate agency. You could use your Facebook page to share helpful content with people who are moving house. For example, post useful articles giving advice on how to present your home to prospective buyers.

Or, a checklist people can review to ensure they've got everything covered during the process. This shows that your company understands the needs of your customers. Plus, you have the expert knowledge to help them make moving their house easier.

Simon Says: "By creating valuable content and then linking the content through social media, you can establish yourself as the go-to source in your field."

It Helps You Provide a More Personal Experience for Your Customers

As a general rule, people enjoy dealing with people. Social Media can help businesses provide a more personal experience for their customers. Larger organisations in particular, sometimes face the challenge of appearing unfriendly or unapproachable.

However, when such companies use social media, it immediately provides an easy route for customers to get in touch with them. It can make people realise the company is run by human beings, and not just automated systems. It helps you build a relationship with your prospects and customers. It's all about making a connection that allows people to feel involved.

It Helps You Listen to What Your Customers Are Saying - and What They Want

This one is a biggie! Social Media provides you with a wonderful opportunity to easily gain an insight into what your customers are saying. These are comments about your business and what people within your market want.

For example, you can try posting various pieces of content, then track which piece generates the most user interest.

Let's say that you provide online training to people who are looking to lose weight. You regularly post health and fitness tips to your Facebook page. You then encourage people to comment and upload their photos of their successes. Afterward, their posts are shared amongst their audiences.

One day you post a particular piece of advice that generates hundreds of likes and comments. Where conversely, you would perhaps normally only get maybe ten or twenty comments.

Bingo! You've hit upon something people want to know more about. You then decide to do a whole series of posts following on the original piece of content. Each of these posts also proves to be extremely popular. Therefore you decide to bring to market an entire training course based around that one particular topic.

Social Media can also help you improve your products or services, just by listening to people's experiences. You might notice many of your followers are commenting on your Facebook page about your product. They're saying they like it, but they wish that it had X feature.

You had no idea your customers wanted such a feature. However, the sheer number of people saying the same thing is surprising. It then makes you aware; this is something that is highly important to people within your market. You then modify the product to include that particular feature then you immediately notice an increase in sales.

Some Things to Bear in Mind When Using Social Media

Simon Says: "Why not create downloadable e-books or a white paper that'll be helpful to your audience? You can then link to these from your social media profiles."

Before we get into the nitty-gritty of the different networking sites, it's worth looking at some of the various principles. There are certain aspects you should consider when using them in your business. By following these guidelines, you stand a much greater chance of seeing success with your online activities.

Post Interesting and Relevant Information They Won't Find Anywhere Else

Social Media sites are very busy places, with millions of businesses competing for the attention of their users. For this reason, it is important for businesses to try and stand out from the crowd. One of the best ways of doing this is to be original. Post interesting, relevant and valuable information people won't find anywhere else.

In order to be successful, you have to give people a reason to follow you. You have to engage people with content they're going to find useful, insightful, or even funny. Sadly, this is something of which too many businesses fail.

If you take a look at a selection of social media profiles, you'll find most businesses are boring. They post the same type of updates as their competitors. Many comments are often irrelevant, unhelpful, and are more of a disservice, than of any value. Quite honestly, you can't afford to make this mistake if you want to be successful in this arena.

Become the 'Go-To' Page for Knowledge and Information Regarding Your   Product, Service and Industry

Continuing from the previous point . . . , by posting useful and relevant content to social media, it's possible to establish yourself as an expert in your field. You then become THE 'go-to' source for knowledge and information in your specialised area.

Take the earlier example of a real estate agent who uses social media to share information. He or she can provide tips and advice to make the process of selling and moving easier. By posting this type of information, people are going to see the agent as somebody who is there to help them. Therefore, they are likely to stand out from their competitors who simply post details of properties for sale.

Remember, it is important to give people a reason to follow and engage in your business. Providing outstanding content conveys to people, "Hey, this business knows what they are talking about. They are here to help me, so I'm going to check them out."

Remember, content doesn't have to be posted directly to social media. It is usually better to write short, concise posts and then link to a page on your website for a full report. It could also include images and all the relevant information in more detail.

Simon Says: "Use visual imagery within your social media campaigns. Posts containing pictures are clicked on, up to 5% more than posts without visual content."

Don't Try to Sell on Social Media – It's for Building Rapport and Relationships

Too many businesses use their social media profiles to promote their products and services directly. They hope people will simply click on their content and make a purchase. Although it is indeed an excellent place to find potential new clients and customers, your social profiles are typically not used for direct selling, if at all.

People aren't going to look favourably on a Twitter profile that constantly feeds links to different products in an online store. There are some exceptions to this - for example, informing your customers about a new product launch, or telling them about an upcoming sale.

In addition, you could use an app like Shopify to set up an online store under a different tab on your Facebook Page. However, the difference is you wouldn't try to sell directly from your main Facebook page.

Social Media is primarily about sharing content, building rapport and establishing relationships. It's okay to promote yourself from time to time, but it definitely shouldn't be the focus of your online activities. If you follow this advice, then you should find the actually 'selling' aspect, basically takes care of itself.

Don't Make it All About Your Company – Discuss New Upcoming Developments, Relevant Industry News and Give Your Opinions

One of the biggest mistakes businesses make on social media, is having it all be about their company. They will make endless posts informing people of how wonderful their merchandise is, and how exciting that X, Y and Z products are in the pipeline. However, they fail to recognise that their company isn't the centre of the universe.

Instead, they should be talking about their industry as a whole. By linking and sharing relevant industry news, discussing upcoming developments, etc., it's both useful and beneficial to your audience. At the same time, it demonstrates to people that your business understands, and is in touch with the industry. Again, it is about establishing yourself as a source of *authority*.

Make It Personal

Too many businesses hide behind a corporate façade. However, that's completely the wrong way to approach social media. Rather, you should be using social sites to allow your followers to get to know you and your company.

The content on these sites shouldn't be too personal, but it should be enough to make them feel they know you and your company more intimately. That will help build a bond and reciprocity, thus making them loyal customers.

Try to Add Humour

Social Media is designed to be fun. Therefore it's important to not make all of your posts too serious. While it's important not to go overboard, there can be no denying people enjoy occasional levity. By injecting a little humour into some of your posts, it can make your business seem much more real and approachable. People are more likely to read your updates if they know your content has elements of entertainment as well. It'll make people much more inclined to share your content with others.

Do Not Post if You Have Nothing of Value to Say

One of the biggest misconceptions many people have regarding social media is they should continuously post. The reality is, you should take the opposite approach and only post when you have something of value to say. Trust me, people will soon get sick and tired when they're newsfeeds are bombarded with constant and needless posts.

This is particularly true if these posts have little to no value to the person receiving them. If you have twenty beneficial things to share with your followers on a certain day, then, by all means, do it. But don't just decide, "I'm going to make twenty posts to my Facebook page every day." just for the sake of it.

Make Them Feel Special

Remember, actively maintaining social networks, is always a choice. However if people don't like what you post, they can just as easily un-follow you to stop receiving your updates. So, when people have taken the time and effort to follow you, then it pays to thank them for doing so.

This means making your followers feel special. Examples could be: acknowledging them before anyone else, give them advance notice on new product launches, or giving them priority access to services and discounts. By making people feel special, you will engage your audience more so, and you'll make them feel you care, and they are your priority.

What Do Businesses Using Social Media Need to Be Aware Of?

Social Media can be invaluable with marketing your business. However, there are other aspects of which you need to be mindful:

Social Media Provides an Opportunity for People to Criticise You

Even though this medium can help you build relationships with customers, you also need to be aware that it can easily expose you to criticism. People can very openly express their dissatisfaction towards you and your business. Therefore, the manner in which you deal with this will be crucial to your overall success. As we have already mentioned, it is possible to turn these events into positives outcomes.

Don't Annoy People or Cause Offence When You Post

Even if you try your absolute best to provide relevant, useful content to your audience, you may still annoy certain people. It can be quite difficult to please everyone 100% of the time. Therefore, it's imperative to be as courteous, respectful, and considerate every time you comment. Always take that extra second to consider what you're going to say before hitting that keyboard. This philosophy will pay off in spades more than most people realise.

Social Media Doesn't Provide All the Answers

You should be aware of the fact that using this platform isn't a 'magic pill.' It won't be able to solve all of your marketing problems. Rather, it should just be one facet of a wider marketing strategy that fits into the overall operations of your business. If you lack direction, or your service is rubbish, then social media isn't going to solve your problems.

Engagement Takes Time

I've come across business owners who think successful social networking, simply means signing up to Facebook and Twitter then making a few sporadic posts. The reality is, being successful with online networks means *engaging* your audience. It's important to understand this takes time and isn't just going to happen overnight.

Summary Points

- Almost all businesses should be using social media for increased exposure and engagement. Consistent participation in such sites is highly likely to increase as a result. The people who don't use it, however, will miss out on a huge opportunity.

- Its usage should be part of a wider marketing strategy.
- There are many benefits when using it appropriately. It can help you find new customers, build relationships, increase trust, improve customer service, gain valuable feedback and more.

- If it is implemented in the correct way, it doesn't require a great amount of time, effort and money.

- To be successful, it is necessary to take a long-term approach.

- It is important to be aware of various issues that may arise and to know how to deal with them accordingly.

5. What Are the Main Social Media Networks?

Over the years the number of social networking sites has greatly increased. Many of them have a distinct focus, different purposes, and a unique set of features. Each networking platform also has its benefits, strengths, weaknesses, and aspects, of which you should be aware.

Before we begin, it's worth noting that no single social site provides the complete set of solutions for a business. Most companies will likely use a mixture of the different platforms. However, that doesn't mean they should be using every single network.

The most practical and effective answer is, most businesses should prioritise and concentrate on only certain sites. This is based on components such as their objectives and whom they're trying to target through their activities. This is something we'll discuss in more detail later on.

In addition, it is also important to note, each platform has distinct elements in the way they function. Each site also has a different type of user base and distinct styles of interaction. Sites such as Reddit and Pinterest, for example, have a more specific focus and appeal to certain groups.

For instance, a site like Pinterest typically appeals to female decorators, craftspeople, cooks, and designers. Whereas a site like Facebook, has a much wider user base that caters to numerous groups and industries. A single person will likely use it for various purposes because he or she can contact people within different social circles.

Certain sites are, of course, used by a variety of people at different times. For example, somebody might regularly use Facebook and YouTube in the evenings and on weekends. Conversely, Linkedin might be a site they use more in the daytime when they're at work.

Additionally, using multiple platforms at the same time is commonplace. Someone may take a photo on Instagram, for example, and then share it to their Facebook and Twitter profiles. They can do this by using the share feature in the Instagram app. In the same way, a user might watch or post a YouTube video and then share it on Facebook.

Another important differentiator between the various social sites is the type and duration of interactions which take place. Some sites are very interactive and create long-lasting conversations between users. However, on other sites such as Reddit, conversation are much shorter.

Someone may post an image, video or article; then users vote it up or down. Perhaps they may make a comment or two, but the conversation doesn't typically continue. Any further interactions between those same users are not as likely to occur. People who interact with each other on Facebook, are much more likely to continue interacting with that same user again in the future.

Facebook

Facebook is always a good place to begin, as it's the largest social network on the planet. It is probably the most mainstream, and it encompasses a broader range of industries. More people are members of Facebook than any other social network today.

What Is It and How Does It Work?

Launched in February 2004, Facebook was the brainchild of Harvard University students Mark Zuckerberg, Eduardo Saverin, Dustin Moskovitz, Chris Hughes, and Andrew McCollum. The site started out as a place for university students to interact with each other. This included its membership initially being limited just to other students of Harvard University.

Soon afterwards, the site grew to include students attending other universities across the United States and Canada. By late 2006, Facebook was launched into the mainstream and became open to anyone with an email address.

According to Facebook itself, the site exists to help you, "Connect and share with the people in your life." Once users are registered, they create their personal profile and then begin adding other Facebook users. This included friends and family who become their "Facebook friends" (contacts).

In addition, Facebook allows users to join groups of people with similar interests (any user can set up their own public or private group). They can also follow groups and pages of organisations, celebrities, and a plethora of other people and entities.

At the heart of Facebook is their *newsfeed*. This is essentially a continually updated feed of topics that shows what users' contacts have been doing. If a person adds a new photograph, for example, it will appear on their contacts' newsfeed.

If a friend updates their status or posts a message, the same thing happens. The newsfeed enables users to see their contacts' activities at any given time, and thus makes it easy to stay in touch.

Today, Facebook is the largest social networking site in the world. Statista's records indicate the site had 1.32 billion users in the

___

second quarter of 2014 and now in early 2016 there are more than 1.55 billion accounts registered. That's a staggering number of users. When you consider Facebook had *just* 100 million users in 2008, you can see just how quickly the site has grown into what it is today.

Why Has Facebook Become So Popular?

We mentioned a little earlier that the king of mainstream social networking websites used to be MySpace. If you're familiar with and can remember MySpace, you'll recall it allowed users the opportunity to customise their profiles. You could upload different templates, backgrounds, and fonts, to create your unique *space*. This proved very popular amongst teenagers at the time.

Facebook took a totally different approach to MySpace, with a limited scope for users to modify their profile. It was much more *grown up*, whereas MySpace profiles were often an unreadable mess. It had clashing backgrounds and fonts that would make any designer run away in horror. Facebook profiles were uncluttered in contrast. They contained all the information people ever needed to know about somebody at a glance.

As well as profiles, Facebook also had a newsfeed, which made it easy to see what your contacts were up to. For example, you could post a status update or share a photo. It would then appear in the newsfeed of all your contacts. This is so that they could see what you were doing.

Facebook also introduced the idea of apps. These allowed third-party developers to create games and other fun programs, which could run on the Facebook platform. As people started to get bored of customising their MySpace profiles, many people started to move over to Facebook.

Once your friends started transitioning over, you wouldn't have wanted to be the one left behind, would you? Remember we're talking about social networking sites here. In order for people to be *social*, you need to be active on the same website as the people with whom you want to keep in touch.

Who Uses Facebook?

Individuals, as well as commercial and charitable organisations, use Facebook. In terms of user age groups, people between 25 to 34 years old make up the biggest proportion. That's approximately 29% of its members using the site.

What Can Facebook Do for My Business?

Facebook provides many opportunities for businesses to find new customers and build relationships with existing ones.

Businesses can use Facebook to:

- Communicate and share relevant content with existing customers and prospects
- Promote their products and services to present and future customers
- Seek out and market to new customers
- Build their brand
-
  . . . and much more.

Facebook can be a great way to find new customers, and promote oneself to existing ones as well. It can certainly help you increase engagement, and build a strong relationship with both present potential new customers.

Facebook Fan Pages

Let's begin by discussing Facebook fan pages. Facebook allows businesses to create a fan page for their company, which contains basic information about the business. It does, however, allow businesses to post regular updates to their respective page(s).

Essentially, a fan page is a bit like an individual's profile. However, it does have some significant differences. To start with, rather than people adding the business as a *friend*, users instead *Like* the page (by clicking the relevant button).

This demonstrates that they want to follow the company. When users *Like* a fan page, the item/s posted by the company will appear on the user's newsfeed. You might, for example, post a news item that links to your website. This will then show people who have 'Liked' your page.

This may work in theory, however, I should also mention that Facebook has started tinkering around with what shows up in people's feeds. This means, although someone may have 'Liked' your page, not all of your updates will appear on their newsfeed.

Facebook introduced this so that users wouldn't see too many posts from one individual or organisation. However, this has reportedly annoyed many users because Facebook is effectively deciding for them, what they do and don't want to see. Regarding businesses, this could be a concerning issue. It serves to demonstrate why you shouldn't measure your success on Facebook, simply by the number of 'Likes' your page has acquired.

Your Facebook page will be the centrepiece of all your activities. You can use Facebook advertising to promote your fan page and also generate *Likes* in that manner. This is to build up a following of people who will engage with your fan page.

Facebook Advertising

Facebook's advertising options are evolving all of the time, and we could take up a whole book on FB advertising techniques and strategies. The following will give you an outline of the sort of promotions that can be done with FB paid marketing

In the main, Facebook offers three main advertising options:

- Adverts and promoted posts within the desktop newsfeed
- Adverts and promoted posts within the mobile newsfeed
- Adverts in the right-hand column of Facebook

Advertisements can point visitors towards either your Facebook fan page, an external website, e-commerce site, an offer or a landing page. It depends on exactly what you are trying to achieve with the advertising campaign. When you create your advertisement, Facebook will ask you for the specific goal to which you are aiming with the campaign. For example, generating sales on your website, or getting people to *Like* your page. This is so you can build your brand and create engagement through targeted content.

Promoted Posts

Promoted posts are slightly different to advertisements. A promoted post is essentially, a regular post you pay to expose to more people than it would otherwise reach. You can, for example, promote posts to people who have similar interests to your page's content, but who don't currently *Like* your page per se.

You can also promote posts to people whom already *Like* your page, but who otherwise might not get to see it. Facebook has changed the way it presents posts to followers in recent years. Unfortunately, this means only a percentage of people who *Like* your page, will see any given post. Research by Social@Ogilvy has put *organic reach*, (the number of people who see the post without paid promotion), at 6% in February 2014.

Furthermore, you can also use promoted posts to ensure users see that content multiple times over the period of a campaign. This can greatly increase the chances of your audience engagement, and taking action on your most important messages.

Facebook Offers

An additional option is to use Facebook Offers. Offers in a similar way to a promoted post. You can choose to show your followers a particular or number of special offers. They will appear in their newsfeed with a *Get Offer* button beside the post. In order to encourage more people to see this, you can also set it up so whoever claims the offer, can share it with their Facebook friends.

Facebook Advertising Targeting Options

One of the weaknesses of traditional advertising options is you can't control who sees your advert. An advert placed in a national newspaper, for example, would certainly reach a large audience. However, that is of little use if 95% of readers aren't actually within your target market.

Businesses have always been able to reach certain audiences, by targeting their advertising and marketing campaigns accordingly. That is, to appear on various media platforms. Platforms they believe are viewed by the type of people, to whom of which they're aiming. It has always been tricky to *only* reach a certain subset of people.

As an example, imagine a company that wants to target teenagers who are interested in playing tennis. An advert in a tennis magazine would enable them to reach that audience. However, not all readers of the magazine will be teenagers.

Now let's take a look at Facebook advertising, which allows you to control who sees your adverts, and when they see them.

Facebook targeting options using their customised audience feature, allows you to select specifically who sees your adverts. This is based on information contained within their Facebook account. Additionally, since Facebook collects such a vast amount of information, you can then reach a very specific subsection of people.

Let's say you want to target thirty-something females who are married, live in New York, and are interested in yoga. You can choose to show your adverts **only** to Facebook users who meet such criteria. You can even target adverts based on user behaviours. For example, people who have recently purchased a particular kind of product, or people who access Facebook using an iPhone.

Although users are often perplexed about the amount of information Facebook collects from its users, this is obviously great for business owners. I hope you can see how powerful this is. This also makes it easier for you to reach a very specific audience of your choice.

You can use this form of targeting which also allows you to reduce your ad spend. This will ensure you aren't spending money, by reaching people who aren't a suitable fit for your specific audience.

You can target adverts towards people based on three main categories:

- Demographics
- Interests
- Behaviours

You can even choose to target people who live in a specific country or even a particular city. Within that area, you might decide you only want to focus on males aged between 18 and 24. Or, who have a specific interest that's closely matched to your subject or niche.

By making your targeting as specific as possible, you'll generate the best results with minimal expenditures. You can even choose the days and the times your advert will be shown. This could be useful for reaching people whom you know spend a lot of time on Facebook, at a particular time of day.

Simon Says: "Do not underestimate the value of targeting."

Let's delve a little deeper into Facebook Targeting, as it is one of the most important and impressive marketing tools the site offers.

Demographics

Facebook allows you to target people who are within a very specific demographic profile.

Demographic categories offered on Facebook are:

- Relationship
- Education
- Work
- Financial
- Home
- Ethnicity
- Generation
- Parents
- Politics (US)
- Life events

Within these categories, there are many subset options that allow you to get specific about who you want to reach. Under *relationships,* for example, you can target people based on whether they're single, in a relationship, civil union, domestic partnership, married, or engaged, etc.

Interests

Facebook targeting goes much deeper than just basic information about the user. One of the most powerful features is the ability to aim towards people who have specific interests.

As an example, you could choose to target people who have *golf* listed as an interest in their profile.

You can even focus on audiences who already *Like* a specific page. So, if you wanted to reach people who have an interest in cars, for example, you could choose to target people who already *Like* the Top Gear Facebook page.

Behaviours

Another very interesting option offered by Facebook is behavioural targeting. This allows you to target ads based on user's actions, or past purchase behaviour. It uses data collected by third parties.

You can target users' behaviour based on the following categories:

- Automotive
- Charitable donations
- Digital activities
- Financial
- Mobile device user

- Purchase behaviour
- Residential profiles
- Travel

Within each category, you have the option to target your advert based on a wide range of users' behaviour.

Take the *mobile device* category for example. You'll see you can choose to target your adverts towards people using a specific mobile operating system, or device. You could also target people who use IOS devices, or just people using Androids. Additionally, you could opt to go much further than this, by targeting people who access Facebook using an iPhone, or people with an iPad.

Success with Targeting Options

Hopefully, you can see how powerful Facebook advertising targeting options are. However, this will only work if you know your target audience. It is essential to know as much about them as possible. The more you're informed about them, the more success you will see with Facebook advertising.

What Are the Advantages of Using Facebook?

Facebook is an extremely popular platform that has many benefits for businesses.

<u>1 Billion+ Members</u>

The first benefit has to be the sheer number of people who use Facebook. Every type of person you can think of is on this site. They range from computer game addicted teenagers, through to senior citizens with unusual interests.

Well Known

Another key advantage of using Facebook is quite simply; it is extremely well known. Therefore, it's certainly becoming true that people expect your business to be using it.

Free to Set Up

Facebook offers the advantage that it's free to set up. You can choose to spend money promoting your business, through various advertising options discussed earlier. However, it costs absolutely nothing for you to sign up and to create a Facebook Page. The good news is that it's an extremely easy process to follow. Facebook guides you through the procedures and the various options it provides businesses.

What Are the Disadvantages of Using Facebook?

Facebook isn't perfect by any means, and there are a few disadvantages you need to be aware of when promoting your business.

You Don't Have Full Control

Perhaps one of the most obvious disadvantages of Facebook, is you don't have full control of its functions and capabilities. You are limited by the way the site is set up to operate. For example, there are certain ways you can customise your Facebook page, but you have to keep the basic layout and structure of the page.

Regular Changes

Facebook is infamous for making regular changes to the way they do things. They often update their user policy, to dictate what is and isn't allowed. Quite honestly, it can sometimes be hard for even the most social media savvy person to keep up with all the changes.

Furthermore, Facebook often adjusts things in the manner in which profiles and posts are displayed. This seems to be a constant frustration amongst certain users. Plus, it can make it challenging for businesses to decide on an effective strategy. What worked well one week, might not work well the next due to such revisions.

Rented Not Owned

Perhaps one of the biggest disadvantages of Facebook is, you don't own your FB pages, nor any of the posts contained within. You have to be careful not to go against or violate their terms of use. These are not complicated, but they don't like you trying to game their system. Violating their terms and conditions, could lead to having your account deleted.

Posts Do Not Reach All of Your Followers Unless You Pay

As previously mentioned, one of the most recent controversial changes, was Facebook's decision to limit the number of your followers who will see your posts. Those who have *Liked* your page won't necessarily see all of your posts. That is unless you pay Facebook, and use their *promoted post* to display them.

This clearly annoys businesses, because they may build a following of thousands of people only to find most of their followers aren't seeing their posts. Many individual users find this vexing.

The reason being, Facebook is essentially deciding what they see and don't see. Many people would argue that if they've taken the trouble to *Like* a page, they most definitely want to see all of the content on that particular page.

Of course, Facebook is a commercial enterprise. Therefore it has to make a profit. So while it's exasperating, (controversial policy changes included) it still offers a cost-effective way to reach your prospects and customers.

One strategy is, to make sure you run a campaign to harvest the email addresses of your customers. In turn, you can then contact them directly outside of Facebook. This can prove highly effective, and it's something more businesses are increasingly using to their advantage.

Twitter

Twitter is also one of the most popular social media platforms available. It can provide a fantastic way to create a following for your business, and increase engagement levels by sharing useful content.

What Is It and How Does It Work?

Twitter was created in 2006 by founder Jack Dorsey. Although, there were also several other people involved in the project, including Noah Glass, Evan Williams and Biz Stone. Originally, it was called Twttr, rather than Twitter, as it is now known. The original idea behind the site was, it provided a way for people to keep track of others' activities via an SMS text messaging style platform.

According to Twitter itself, the site exists to help you, "Connect with your friends - and other fascinating people. Get in-the-moment updates on the things which interest you, and watch events unfold, in real time, from every angle."

Twitter is essentially what is known as a micro-blogging platform. Once users have signed up for an account, they can then post *tweets*.

These are simply short messages containing 140 characters or less. Every tweet the user makes appears on their profile, with the newest one always at the top of the profile. Users can also *follow* other Twitter members and see all of that person's tweets on their home screen.

Additionally, users can communicate with others, by including @username within the tweet (you would replace *username* with the name of the person you want to see the tweet).

Twitter has a home screen that shows you the tweets of all the people you follow. It makes it easy to see what these people are tweeting about, without actually visiting their respective profiles. Essentially this works very much like the Facebook newsfeed. It's a continually updated feed of tweets, where the newest message appears at the top.

Furthermore, if the user is *mentioned* within a tweet (by another user including @theirusername within the tweet), the user will be notified. The tweet will then appear in a separate tab showing *user mentions*.

Finally, users can place #hashtags within a tweet. This tags the tweet with a particular subject. As an example, a tweet about somebody Christmas shopping may include the hashtags #Christmas #Shopping #Crowds or #Liverpoolfc. People can click on hashtags to see tweets by other users, who are talking about the same subject.

Why Are People So Interested In Twitter?

Many experts agree, that the success and appeal of Twitter has a lot to do with one's desire to know other people's activities at any given time. Twitter also allows you to follow the tweets from people who have similar interests. This even can include people who are in the public eye, such as celebrities.

You can follow any other Twitter user you wish. However, there's no obligation for the other person to approve you as a follower, or *add you as a friend*. Any tweet made is completely public, and can be seen by anyone in the world who has access to the internet.

Essentially, it gives people a direct line to celebrities, pop stars, politicians, sports stars, and other famous people. It also allows these people in the public eye, to interact with their fans and share information with them instantly. Although to the chagrin of some celebrities, they have regretted some of their off-the-cuff tweets.

Who Uses Twitter?

In early 2016, Twitter had approximately 320 million monthly active users, sharing 650 million tweets every day. This is quite a staggering figure. The user base incorporates everyone from private individuals, celebrities, and other public figures. This massive base also includes countless businesses and charitable organisations.

What Can Twitter Do for My business?

Similar to Facebook, Twitter provides many opportunities for businesses to find new customers and build engagement with existing ones.

Businesses can use Twitter to:

- Share relevant content with existing customers and prospects
- Interact and communicate, to include promoting their products and services
- Find and market to new customers
- Build their brand

- Listen to, comment, and contribute on what's happening within the market in which they're operating

. . . and much more.

Twitter is particularly helpful for listening to what is occurring within one's industry. Likewise, it's advantageous with discovering what topic(s) interests people. You can see what your competitors are tweeting about, and learn from your followers, which subjects are important to them.

Looking at it from a promotional perspective, one of the key characteristics about Twitter is that tweets are restricted to 140 characters or less. Therefore, it is primarily a platform for talking to other users and linking to content that's been posted somewhere else (e.g., a website or blog).

On Facebook, for example, you could post an entire article to your fan page. Whereas on Twitter, you are limited to just posting the title or a short comment about an article. This would also include a hyperlink to a site where people can go to read the full article.

Twitter is also beneficial for creating a viral effect. Popular tweets can get *retweeted* thousands of times. This is where other users post someone else's tweet to their own profile. A retweet by somebody who has thousands of followers means your business can be placed in front of those masses of other Twitter users. Fortuitously, some of those said users, may, in turn, decide to follow you.

Twitter Advertising

Twitter offers three main advertising options:

- Promoted tweets. These allow you to put tweets in front of people who don't yet follow you.

- Promoted accounts. This option puts your account in front of targeted people who haven't yet found you.
- Promoted trends. This encourages people to talk about a certain #hashtagtopic.

What Are the Advantages of Using Twitter?

Twitter has many advantages as an effective medium to market your business.

<u>271 Million Monthly Active Users</u>

Twitter is used by millions of people every day. Many popular accounts have tens of thousands or even millions of individual followers. It is, therefore, possible to gain massive exposure through Twitter, and more beneficially, for your tweets to go *viral*.

<u>Every Tweet Is Shown to Your Followers</u>

Unlike Facebook, every tweet you make will appear on the home screen of your followers. Meaning, you know all of your followers are at least having a chance of seeing your tweets. That doesn't necessarily suggest that they will see every tweet of course. Sometimes people are following hundreds, if not thousands of people on Twitter. This implies that new tweets are appearing on their home screen every few seconds.

<u>Users Actively Follow Businesses</u>

Twitter quotes a <u>study</u> by the website Compete, which found users on average, follow six or more brands on Twitter.

They follow brands to:

- Find discounts and promos
- Get free stuff
- Engage in fun and entertainment
- Get updated on upcoming sales
- Get access to exclusive content

Well Known

Twitter is one of the most well-known social media platforms, consisting of an immense spectrum of users. Due to this, people have come to expect your business will be on Twitter.

Free to Set Up and Has a Small Learning Curve

Twitter provides you with an option to advertise, where you can pay money to promote your tweets to a wider audience. It's completely free to create a Twitter account and start posting tweets. Twitter is quite a simple concept and once you've grasped it, it has a relatively small learning curve.

It Encourages You to Keep Your Messages Short and Simple

I've heard some people say they felt limited by Twitter's 140-character limit. However, in many ways, it's considered an advantage. It encourages you to get *straight to the point* and to avoid fluffy marketing messages with no meaning, nor value. A short tweet can have real impact, and it gets users to take action. Eg: *click on a link within the tweet, which then takes the user to your website's landing page.*

What Are the Disadvantages of Using Twitter?

Twitter has a few disadvantages—and it is certainly worth bearing these in mind:

Twitter Is Extremely Busy

The huge popularity of Twitter is both a blessing and a curse. The vast number of users and daily tweets indicate Twitter is indeed a thriving community. Now granted, it does have the potential to help you reach a massive audience. However, its sheer volume of tweets can mean your messages may get lost in the crowd.

Many of your contacts will also be following hundreds or even thousands of others on Twitter. Therefore, even though your tweets will appear on their home screens, there's no guarantee they will see them.

Those who follow a high number of users will learn that their home screen has new tweets appearing every few seconds. This can occur within minutes, so your tweet will be buried below hundreds of others.

To Get Noticed You Need to Tweet Throughout the Day

To get noticed on Twitter, you need to be posting throughout the day for maximum efficacy. Perhaps even making the same tweet multiple times, that is, to capture more of the people whom it might engage.

If your marketing strategy is not properly managed, Twitter can become a burden on time and resources. Thankfully, there are certain tools available such as HootSuite and Rignite. These can help businesses to take control and simplify their Twitter activities.

You Can Only Make Tweets of 140 Characters or Less

We covered this in the advantages section, however, it can also be a disadvantage. Some people find the 140-character rule to be rather limiting. It can be a problem when you're trying to convey a difficult concept or message, requiring additional words. Your comment may need further explanation for example, in order for people to better understand the crux of your message.

Instagram

What Is It and How Does It Work?

Instagram is a photo and video-sharing app. It is dedicated to mobile phones and tablet devices and was established in 2010. Facebook then purchased Instagram in 2012, for $1 billion!

If you're not familiar with Instagram, it is somewhat similar to Twitter (quick, snappy posts). However, its sole concept revolves around posting photographs and videos. Users can follow other Instagram users, who then receive that person's photographs on their screens.

People can comment on photos and, as with Twitter, you can include @username in your comment when interacting with others. Instagram also supports #hashtags. Therefore, users can tag their photos with subjects and topics. Subsequently, they can then click on those #hashtags to find other photos about the same subject. Unlike Twitter, you are not limited to 140 characters in the comments section.

Hashtags play a very important role in Instagram and other social media sites as they allow people to search out posts and tweets related to their interests. Always tag your photo or video with relevant hashtags to make it easier, for others that are interested in your subject, product or service, to find you

What makes Instagram so popular is, it allows users to take photographs using their smartphone or camera-enabled mobile device. They can then easily edit their photos and share them with other people instantly. These people can be both Instagram followers and others on various social platforms.

Users can add a selection of filters to their photographs as well. They can do things such as adjust the lighting, change contrast levels, and crop their images. It is extremely intuitive and allows anyone to take a photograph, make it look professional, and then share it with other people.

Who Uses Instagram?

Instagram has a younger demographic, 90% of its users are younger than 35. However, it has seen phenomenal growth since its inception. By December of 2010, the site acquired 1 million users. This grew to 5 million in June 2011, and they had passed 10 million by September of the same year. It had grown to more than 300 million in December of 2014. By this time, there were an astonishing 60 photos per second being uploaded. In September of 2015, Instagram had more than 400 million active monthly users with 75 million users per day.

This makes it a very powerful way of getting your message out there, and more and more business owners are getting in on the act!

What Can Instagram Do for My Business?

Instagram isn't the first social media platform one would think of when it comes to promoting a business. But, it certainly can be used as an integral part of your marketing strategy nonetheless. It can be particularly useful if your products are visually appealing.

For example, if your business is creating unique handmade gifts, then you might post images of the latest items you're presently creating. A builder might post photos of his work in progress or before and after pictures. Another example would be a travel company using Instagram to share photographs of the various destinations where they offer holiday packages.

Any graphic file can be uploaded to the site. Therefore, different styles of graphics, drawings, as well as adding text to photos, are all possible. Doing so will be of great benefit to your sales, promotions and messages to your viewers.

You cannot add links to Instagram posts, only in your profile, so adding a watermark of your website or company name or product can help get your brand name out there.

What Are the Advantages of Instagram?

One of the main benefits is the expansive audience you can reach, plus, it's free to use. It has a clean interface, and its navigational features are user-friendly. It only does one thing, and that is share images. As a result, people don't get lost or side-tracked in long threads or conversations.

Images are delivered directly to users' devices, and they can scroll through countless photos if they so choose. It is much easier to make an image stand out, compared to a text message or a tweet. If you can make your photo grab the attention of people as they scroll through their account, your chances are greatly increased that it's noticed. Afterwards, your image is shared or, better still, goes viral.

Instagram also gives you an extended reach. It's very easy to combine it with your marketing activities on other networking platforms. You can post a photograph or video to Instagram, and then share it via the Instagram app. It can go directly to your

Facebook fan page and/or Twitter account. This method can provide you, even more, exposure.

Instagram recently (2015) introduced paid advertising that allows companies to promote posts to the huge number of Instagram members.

Instagram adverts are setup through Facebook's advertising power editor, which allows you to drill down to a very specific demographic. **For more details** – *refer to the section on Facebook advertising*

What Are the Disadvantages of Instagram?

The images are restricted to being square, and videos are limited to only 15 seconds long (or 30 seconds for promoted, paid for videos).

You cannot add links to the posts, only to your profile page. You can, however, add text your photos and images, which enables you to add your brand name, website or company email for example.

Snapchat

Snapchat was the brainchild of Evan Spiegel and Reggie Brown and was conceived as project when the two were at Stanford University.

Snapchat is a relatively new player to the social media market having launched in 2011 however, it should not be ignored.

What Is It and How Does It work?

Snapchat allows users to take photos and create videos and broadcast them on to 'My Story', a daily diary or directly to other users.
They are curated throughout the day and played in chronological order.

Snapchat is a messaging app that allows users to users to take photos and videos, add captions, doodles, masks and special lenses onto them before adding them to 'My Story" or directly to other snapchat users. These images and videos are only online for a 24 hours, after that they disappear.

When you click on someone's story, each image is displayed for up to a maximum of 10 seconds (you choose in settings) and then automatically shows the next image or 10 second video clip.

A more recent feature allows you to store memories, which remain until the user deletes them.

Bringing Fun to Social Media

One of the features of Snapchat is the ability to add funny masks and overlays onto your video as well as voice changers and even face swapping. When you touch and hold your finger on a face in the camera, a selection of masks Oakes Energy Services Limited lenses as snapchat call them appears which have different effects. Raising your eyebrows or opening your mouth can activate some, others appear as scroll through them.

Who Uses Snapchat?

Teens and young adults particularly favoured it in the early days and it became known as the app to send daring or sometimes intimate photos, knowing, that after being viewed, these images would disappear.
This did, however, caused controversy, when it was discovered how easy it was to capture and store the images and they could in fact be kept.

Although it started out popular with the younger generation, it has fast been adopted by a lot of celebrities, major brands, magazines and news media companies who now have their own curated channels and content.

One thing to remember is that there is a pattern with social media platforms. They all start off with a younger audience but over time these platforms are adopted by the older demographic.

Even my 78-year-old Mother is on Facebook now and I am sure she is nowhere near the oldest or the only one.

Take note now and get involved now.

How Big Is Snapchat?

Snapchat has seen a growth of over 350% in a year!

As of June 2016 Snapchat had more that 150 million people using the app daily, with people viewing and watching over 10 billion photos and videos a day, making it more popular than Twitter.

Due to the increase in numbers, the age demographics has now increased but it is still seems primarily as a young person's app and has over took the mighty Facebook in the 12 to 25 year old demographic.

Snapchat Statistics (September 2016)

It grew more in one year than Twitter did in 4 years.
It has more users than Linked, in Twitter or Pinterest
It gets more video views than Facebook or YouTube!

What Are the Advantages of Snapchat?

People love the fact that the information is less than 24 hours old making it perfect to get your messages and news out there.

Like most social media platforms, it allows your business to show a human side, people want to feel personally connected and create a 2-way communication with you and your brand and these mediums allow you to do that.

You can post photos and videos of behind the scenes stuff, things you would NOT post on twitter, Facebook or your blog. It allows people to get to know you and your business on a completely different level.

Unlike Twitter, where all your tweets are stored, and the feed can get very busy or Facebook where the wall has everything on show, Snapchat, by its very nature, only has the freshest and latest information on available making it easy for people to keep up to date with your latest news about your products or services.

People are not interested in yesterday's news or finding out about what they missed. When they view your snapchat they will see your latest offer or updated information and not something that may have been relevant last week.

It also creates urgency, if you post regularly then people need to check in on you on a daily basis.

And, of course they love the fun aspect. Snapchat are constantly bringing in new masks and overlays that people find amusing and keeps users coming back and interacting several times a day on average.

What Can Snapchat Do For My Business?

Used properly Snapchat can have a huge impact on your business.

You do need to be consistent with Snapchat and update regularly. It is good to be creative and fun with your snaps.

It is perfect for conversations and direct communication with your followers and one on one when needed.

More people watched details of the MTV awards on Snapchat than they did on tv.

They reach over 41% of the US population of 18 - 34 year olds as opposed to a tv network which has just a 6% penetration.

Use Snapchat to collaborate with influencers in your World. This will help you build your audience faster.

Snapchat does not make it easy for people to follow you or for you to follow them. You have to go out and find their snapchat username or id code and add it. It is not a simple matter to just click follow or like as you can with other social media platforms.

This means that a lot of companies do not bother so, if you do then you will be ahead of your game.

—

It is a perfect way to share your latest news about products and services.

Let your customers know about a free offers or send out a daily promo code that will give followers a discount or details on today's special offers.

Broadcast updates on a launch or an upcoming event.

You can do this without disappointing those that did not see your post in time.

Snapchat allows you to build excitement and urgency as you do a daily countdown for example.

You can let people know about issues or things that have happened that are funny or interesting or even serious issues.

You can also download your photos or videos from snapchat, if you want to, so you can save them and upload to Instagram, Facebook or Twitter.

Advertising on Snapchat

In 2015 Snapchat launched Discover where you can promote your own video editorial.

You can also use Snap ads where users can interact with your mobile website. They claim to have an average 5 X higher click through rate.

It starts with a 10 second video ad and also gives the user a choice to swipe up to learn more. Swiping up can reveal a full length video, article or even an app install.

Sponsored Geofilters—these filters allow you to take over other people's snaps. When users are in a location of your choosing they will be shown your geofilter over the image or video.

Lenses are a fun way to brighten up your pics and videos. When using a sense and you open your mouth or raise your eyebrows an effect is triggered like fire coming out of your mouth or your eyes turning into giant goggles. You can sponsor your own lenses which is a great way to create viral content. As you can imagine, this is going to set you back some serious amount of money but, if you have the budget, it has proven to be well worth the money.

Remember, the beauty of social media is that you are able to generate, followers, friends and customers for free on all platforms. It just takes work a good strategy and persistence.

What Are The Disadvantages of Using SnapChat?

The fact that your photos and videos are removed after 24 hours can itself be a disadvantage for messages that you want to remain on view.

This means that you have to republish every day although this is not the best use of Snapchat.

You have to use a mobile device to upload photos and video. There is not a desktop version.

Google+

Having launched in 2011, Google+ is relatively new to the social media scene. However thanks to Google's dominance, it has rapidly grown to become the second largest social platform in terms of registered users. Its figures show that 1.15 billion people had a Google+ account in the fourth quarter of 2013.
Of those users, just 35% (359 million) were active members; this could also be an indication, many of those are using other Google properties that are tied in with Google+. It isn't as well known as sites like Facebook, Twitter, and Linkedin. However, when it is used in the right way, it can certainly be a powerful tool to have at your disposal.

What Is It and How Does It Work?

According to Google+, it's a place for people to connect with friends, family, and explore all of their interests. In this way, it is much like any other networking site. However, the way in which it works has some key differences to rival other social networks. This includes several unique features other platforms don't provide.

Let's start with the basics. Each Google+ user has their profile which can be updated at will. This can include the usual profile picture, about me page, etc. Businesses and organisations can create a Google+ page as well.

It works in a similar way to a Facebook page. On this page, businesses can do things like post news updates, share photographs, and post links to external websites. Users who follow you on Google+ will then see this content.

On its home tab, people can view recent posts by the people whom they follow. Subsequently, the most recent updates appear at the top of the page. If you're unfamiliar with Google+, the easiest way to look at it is, it's very much like Facebook's newsfeed.

What Are Google Circles?

Google+ largely revolves around *circles*. They are essentially groups of individuals and organisations that users classify by topic. You can create a circle for friends, a circle for family, for colleagues, and so on. In addition, you can also generate circles for your specific interests.

For example, create a circle for *travel,* and then add individuals, companies, and communities related to travel into that circle. It is possible to add a Google+ user to *multiple* circles. As a result, you may put Adidas into fashion, sports, football, businesses, etc.

There are also special circles called- *following*. These are created by default when a user signs up to Google+. When somebody lands on a Google+ page (as opposed to a personal profile) they will see a +Follow button near the top of the page. This button is then clicked, and then adds the page to the user's *following* circle. Essentially, this is equivalent to *Liking* a page on Facebook.

Why Are People Interested in Google+?

One of the key reasons for the success of Google+ is that it makes it very easy for users to keep track things in which they're most interested. We know that following users on Twitter or Facebook is a wonderful option for keeping tabs on people, places, and things. Google+ makes it much easier to see the things that matter to you most.

Whereas on Twitter, you see tweets from all the people you are following as a whole. You can sign into Google+ however, go to your *travel circle,* and only see updates related to travel. Next, you can go to your *friends'* circle/s and only see their respective updates, and so on.

Additionally, Google+ also has some nifty features that differentiate it from many rival networks. Google+ Hangouts would be an obvious example. Hangouts is a feature which allows you to have live conversations and chats, with up to ten friends. It also includes the option to video chat with each other. It doesn't matter what device people are using during Hangouts. You can have a group hangout with people using Windows, Macs, Android and iOS devices.

From a business perspective, Google+ Hangouts can help you engage with your target audience. It can truly be a useful place to share content with them. Imagine you were a food retailer. You could host a Google+ Hangout where you invite local chefs, share recipe ideas, and invite people to ask questions about cooking. This is one of countless scenarios using this particular medium.

Who Uses Google+?

Although it has similarities to Facebook, Google+ is widely considered to be less 'mainstream.' Seemingly, everyone logs onto Facebook on a daily basis to share news, updates, photos and videos with their friends and family. Google+ however, is a place people go to connect with others whom they don't personally know, but who share common interests.

At the risk of over-generalising, Facebook is where people post funny photographs of their friends, and broadcast details of their love life. Conversely, Google+ is where graphic designers come together to talk about their craft, business owners come to connect and share strategies with each other, and so on.

In terms of raw statistics, figures show 1.15 billion people had a Google+ account in the fourth quarter of 2013. Of those users, just 35% of them (359 million) were considered active.

What Can Google+ Do for My Business?

Google+ can help you build your brand presence, to include Google search results as well. It can help grow and engage your audience with useful content, and help you understand how customers find your brand.

Businesses can use Google+ to:

- Share relevant content with existing customers and prospects
- Interact, communicate, plus promote products and services with said people
- Find and market to new customers
- Build their brand
- Listen to, comment and contribute on what is happening within the market in which they're operating

. . . *and much more.*

Advertising Using Google+

Google+ provides one main advertising option called +Post ads. A +Post ad is a regular Google+ post that's also shown on a website outside of the Google+ site. Let's say your business was a garden centre, and you made a post that shared tips on how to be a better gardener. You could turn this post into a paid +Post ad, which could then be shown on websites related to gardening.

A clever feature is, +Post adverts are interactive within an external website. Therefore, the viewer of the ad can comment on the post, give a +1, or join a Hangout right from the ad itself. This is similar to viewing a regular post within the Google+ website.

+Post ads form part of the Google Display Network. It provides you with the tools to target ads based on demographics, affinity segments, and contextual targeting. In addition, +Post ads are optimised for the device on which it's being displayed. That can be a desktop computer, smartphone, or tablet.

What Are the Advantages of Using Google+?

Although Google+ is perhaps not the first social network that springs to mind, it offers many advantages as a platform to promote your business.

Google+ Is the Second Largest Social Networking Platform . . . and Growing

Despite only 35% of users being active, Google+ has well over 1 billion accounts, which means that it's pretty hard to ignore. There are contradicting opinions about the future of Google+. However, it's probably likely as awareness grows, so will the number of people who use it regularly. Many people would agree Google+ has a lot of untapped potential, so it's a platform you shouldn't be ignoring.

It Helps You to Be Recognised in the Search Engines

One of the main benefits of this platform is, having a strong Google+ presence can help you to be recognised in the search engines. Google indexes status updates immediately. Therefore if a post is shared or gets a +1, for example, it sends a signal to its algorithm. It tells the search engines the content is relevant to people, and thus can rank higher in search results. Although being on Google+ _can't be_ your entire SEO strategy, it definitely should be a part of it.

_Simon Says__: "Optimise your Google+ posts with suitable and relevant keywords."_

Google+ Can Help You Stand Out

Most businesses have a Facebook and/or Twitter account. However, there are far fewer that have an active presence on Google+. By engaging in this network, it is easier to stand out from the crowd and provide something unique in your industry. This is particularly true if you take full advantage of its various components.

Google+ Is Feature-Rich

As we have discussed, Google+ offers several features that make it uniquely distinguishable from other social networks. Take Google+ Hangouts and Google+ Communities for example. These properties could provide you with many opportunities, to engage your audience and gain valuable feedback. Moreover, dynamic +Post advertisements can help you reach people outside of Google+.

What Are the Disadvantages of Using Google+?

Like all the social networks, Google+ also has several weaknesses of which you should be aware.

Google+ Isn't as Popular as Facebook and Twitter

Perhaps the most obvious disadvantage of Google+ is, it isn't yet as widely used as some of the other social platforms. Although Google+ is quite similar to Facebook, in terms of what it was originally designed to do, it isn't close to achieving the same levels of engagement. You probably know many people who check their Facebook and Twitter accounts, almost on an hourly basis. But, how many of them check Google+ every day to see what's going on?

<u>SEO Benefits Have Limitations</u>

There's no doubt Google+ can help you get more content into the search results. However, the actual content doesn't rank as highly, when the person isn't logged into Google services. Google personalises its results that are seen by a user. Therefore, a search result appearing in the number two position by somebody logged into Google, might only be ranked at number 10. This can occur when viewed by somebody who's *logged out* of the Google platform.

Linkedin

Linkedin is considered the most well-known business-oriented social network. In 2014, it had over 300 million users in more than 200 countries and territories. These numbers made it an important player in the world of social media- primarily in the world of B2B (Business to Business).

What Is It and How Does It Work?

Linkedin was founded in 2002 by- Reid Hoffman, Allen Blue, Konstantin Guericke, Eric Ly, and Jean-Luc Vaillant. The site officially launched in May 2003. Unlike other social media platforms, Linkedin is a place specifically designed for connecting professionals. The site describes itself as 'the world's largest professional network.'

According to Linkedin itself, the site exists to, "Connect the world's professionals to make them more productive and successful. When you join Linkedin, you get access to people, jobs, news, updates, and insights, that help you be great at what you do."

When a user signs up for Linkedin, they are firstly asked to create a profile. This is essentially like an online curriculum vitae (CV). The user is required to fill out information, such as their professional summary, job history, and key skills.

Once signed up on the site, people can then use the site to *connect* with other Linkedin professionals. Each association is kept up to date with the professional life of that user. This means when a user connects with another person, they'll be notified of any changes with his/her job, updates their professional skills, gains a new qualification, etc.

As well as connecting with each other, it is also possible to endorse and recommend other users. A company who hires a freelance copywriter, for example, might endorse the user as being skilled in his/her craft. The company can then write a recommendation for the user on their profile (this is basically like a testimonial).

In addition to individual professionals, creating a company profile is also possible. This is where businesses can post updates about their company and connect with their employees. Users can *follow* a company and choose to see its updates. People can then view details on who already works for them, and see information about any current job opportunities.

Linkedin also provides Linkedin Groups. This is where users can come together to talk about a specific industry, share their knowledge, and have questions answered. Linkedin Groups can be an excellent place to network with other professionals. In turn, they can ensure businesses stay in touch with exactly what is happening within their respective industry.

Who Uses Linkedin?

Professionals, businesses, and non-profit organisations from all over the world, use Linkedin to connect with each other. In 2014, the site had over 300 million users, in more than 200 countries and territories.

As previously mentioned, Linkedin is a *professional* network. However, many of these professionals will be active on other social media sites as well. As a result, their Linkedin profile will be very different from what is contained in their Facebook profile, for example.

It is very popular with recruitment companies and head-hunters reaching out to various professionals on the site. The reason being, so many people post their work history, skill set and qualifications, which enables recruiters to seek and find candidates for jobs. This even includes those not currently looking for a new position.

What Can Linkedin Do for My Business?

According to Linkedin, the site helps users to:

- Build a professional identity online
- Stay in contact with colleagues and classmates
- Discover professional opportunities, business deals, and new ventures
- Get the latest news and developments within specific industries
- Source the head buyer or marketing manager for a particular company

One of the main benefits of using Linkedin from a business perspective, it enables companies to network with other businesses. Moreover, so that such companies can seek outside assistance if necessary. We gave the example earlier, regarding the large-buttoned mobile phone company.

This particular company can connect with opticians who may be willing to promote their mobile phone products. This is just one of countless examples. Linkedin can also be advantageous when finding suppliers, contractors, and other people needed to run your business.

It can even provide an effective means of networking with potential joint venture partners. What's more, Linkedin makes it easier to connect with the right people, whom may otherwise be more difficult to reach. Junior office staff, for example, can use Linkedin to network with, and build a connection with the CEO of another organisation.

Even if an individual doesn't personally know somebody with whom they want to connect, they can request to be introduced to that person. This is typically done via another member with whom they have already connected.
Another key benefit when using Linkedin is it provides a substantial source of candidates for jobs. If you are looking to recruit somebody for your company, you can use Linkedin to search for potential applicants.

Typically, those who already possess the skills related to your business. Linkedin profiles are essentially like an online CV. You can easily read through any given profile, and determine whether or not the person is potentially suitable. This is usually based on the skill sets you are looking for.

Linkedin is also very useful for keeping up to date with news, developments, and topical issues within your industry. Need to keep up to date with the latest developments in the UK IT industry? You

---

can then join a related discussion group. Want to connect with other marketing professionals and get ideas for campaigns? Join a Linkedin discussion group for marketing professionals.

Within these groups, you can easily stay in tune with information that's important to the business and its industry. By actively participating in these groups, you can also appear as an expert in your field. This helps people gain a positive impression of your respective organisation and all it entails.

Linkedin Is at Its Best When Everyone in the Company Uses It

Linkedin is less about promoting your company as a whole, and more about staff members making connections with others. Therefore, Linkedin works best when everyone within the organisation, is encouraged to use it to its full potential. Employees can use it to network with other professionals, as well as joining relevant groups. This will enable them to keep up to speed with the latest developments within your industry.

Linkedin Premium Services

Premium Membership

Linkedin offers premium services, which gives the member/s additional benefits.

Sales Navigator

The Linkedin Sales Navigator is a multi-faceted lead generator. It enables users to effectively source leads and prospects. Linkedin has an expansive database of businesses, accessing up to 300 million professional profiles. This includes more than 2 million company pages. Once you add the details of your products or services, Linkedin will search their database and provide you leads tailored to your business. You can save up to 3000 leads at a time.

It also has a *customer relationship manager* so that you can track the progress and sales from these leads. Some businesses solely use Linkedin to generate sales for their company.

Recruitment Services

- Search for a job
- Contact HR directly in a company
- Find and hire talented people

Targeted Advertising

Similar to Facebook, Linkedin has a number of ways to raise awareness about your company, and/or to promote your products and services.

You can create text and image ads, banner ads, video ads, or text only.

- Sponsored Updates - Get your advert seen in the news feeds

- Pay Per Click or (PPC) and Pay Per Impression (PPM) advertising
- B2B Targeting - Job Title, Position, Industry, Geo-targeting, Company size, Seniority, etc.

Simon Says: "Encourage all staff members to sign up for a Linkedin account. Then start using it on a daily basis to keep updated within the industry you operate."

What Are the Advantages of Using Linkedin?

We've already covered some of the ways Linkedin can be used within your business. However, it doesn't do any harm to look at the advantages and disadvantages of this popular social network.

Linkedin Is Well Known with High Numbers of Users

Approximately 300 million people have a Linkedin account. This indicates it has the potential to help you reach out to an abundant number of people. More and more professionals are realising its advantages and benefits. This means that this number is only likely to grow.

What's more, there's a good chance the professionals with whom you want to network, are already using Linkedin. Therefore, when you meet a new contact in person (or through another digital platform) you can immediately add them as a contact. Subsequently, this allows you to build the relationship and stay in touch.

Relationships with Your Staff

Interestingly, Linkedin also gives you the opportunity to be closer and more informed about your employees, and them about you. This is especially true with companies that have a large staff. The fact that people put up their CV and a short biography, allows you to get to know your staff more intimately. More so now, than what you probably would have known before Linkedin existed.

You can go over potential candidates more thoroughly and easily. You can also prioritise people whom you think would be suitable for a promotion, or a new position you want to fill internally.

Simon says: "Remember, people add their CVs and bios to Linkedin whether they are looking for a job or not. This allows you to find talented people and potential staff, whom you would not find through normal recruitment websites."

Checking Out New Suppliers

When looking at new or alternative suppliers for products or services, you can check them out like never before. By using Linkedin (as well as other social accounts like Twitter and Facebook) you'll see how they deal with their customers, and also read the feedback they receive.

Linkedin Guides The User

All social networks are relatively easy to use as a whole. However, Linkedin is particularly strong in this respect. This is because it actively guides the user on how to get the most out of it. When you create a profile or company page, it provides useful messages that tell you the steps you can take to improve your profile.

Members Are More Focused on Business

One of the biggest problems with sites like Facebook is when people log in they're usually thinking about social matters. In turn, businesses have to compete for their attention. If you've ever read the comments left on paid promoted posts on Facebook, you've probably seen statements like, "Why are you trying to sell to me on my timelines?"

People sometimes get annoyed when business advertisements appear on their newsfeed. The reason being, they are more concerned about seeing the latest photos posted by their friends. Linkedin on the other hand is a network for professionals. When people sign into Linkedin, you know without question, they are solely focused on business-related matters.

What Are the Disadvantages of Using Linkedin?

Granted, Linkedin has many advantages and does many things well, but it certainly isn't perfect.

Linkedin Requires Time to Master Its Features

In many aspects, this point applies to all social networking sites. However, the way in which Linkedin works, it can become quite time-consuming if you want to get the most out of it. It relies largely on personal user interaction. This can quickly start to consume large amounts of your time unless it is managed effectively. Performing tasks like posting to Linkedin Groups, answering questions, and interacting with other members, can become tiresome.

Not Everyone Uses Linkedin Every Day

Linkedin boasts 300 million members on its site. However, it is also important to remember, not everyone signs into Linkedin every day. This can mean messages and other user interactions, are left unnoticed until next time the user signs into their account.

Linkedin Has the Potential to Damage Your Reputation

We mentioned earlier, the best way of using Linkedin is to encourage every individual in your business, to use the site on a regular basis. However, this also suggests there is the potential for them to damage your business' reputation.

When employees post content, they are representing your business. Consequently, something as a misguided message in a Linkedin Group could cause problems.

It's imperative to remember, you and your employees are very closely linked, so you should also be careful of the information you post. Make sure the relevant people are informed, before you release a new product or service update to the world.

YouTube

No book on social media would be complete without a look at YouTube. The highly popular video sharing website that is now under ownership by Google. Although there are other video sharing platforms in existence, no other video-focused site has anywhere near the same dominance as YouTube.

What's more, video has exploded in popularity in recent years. Increases in broadband speeds and the introduction of 4G networks have allowed much faster streaming without the dreaded buffering. Video is immense, and should form a part of your social strategy.

What Is It and How Does It Work?

YouTube is a video sharing website that was created in 2005 by three former Paypal employees. Google has owned it since 2006. It presently forms a key segment in Google's network of services.

YouTube allows users to upload, view and share videos with other people. The site integrates with all of the other popular social media networks. Users can easily share a video they uploaded or watched, to other sites such as Facebook.

In addition, YouTube videos are easily shareable on any website. Each video page includes a unique code, which can be copied and pasted onto other websites. Therefore, a video that you uploaded to YouTube can be put directly on your website or blog. The video is embedded into the page, without requiring any special technical skills.

Users can browse through and watch videos on YouTube without requiring an account. However, you will need to create a YouTube profile before you can upload or comment on videos. Anyone who has a Google account already has a YouTube account. When you're signed into other Google services, you'll also be signed into YouTube. What's more, it also integrates with the popular Google+ social network.

YouTube allows users to create Channels. These allow people to create a channel around a particular subject and assemble all of their videos in one place. Users can subscribe to a channel in which they're interested, and then be notified each time a new video is uploaded to that channel.

Who Uses YouTube?

Every person imaginable uses YouTube. These videos have the potential to reach almost any kind of target audience you can conceive. Those familiar with YouTube will also know, the range of videos cover virtually every subject and area of interest out there.

Everything from humour videos, music videos, film trailers, and entertainment are listed. The site also provides in-depth product reviews, news, and step-by-step tutorials. The extent and depth of videos available on YouTube are quite astounding.

It also certainly boasts some pretty impressive usage statistics. More than 1 billion people visit YouTube every single month. Over 6 billion hours of video are watched monthly. YouTube itself, points out this is almost an hour for every person on earth.

You can now really see the wide-ranging appeal of this medium, and how it can help you reach many different people. If someone regularly uses the internet, the chances are they check into YouTube fairly often.

In terms of people who post videos and create YouTube channels, this ranges from individuals, small organisations, through to multinational companies. Some of the biggest brands in the world take full advantage of its popularity and its global user base.

New subscribers who create channels, continually increases dramatically. In 2014, the number of people establishing channels every day rose more than three times since the previous year. Furthermore, the overall number of daily subscriptions has increased more than four-fold over the same period.

What Can YouTube Do for My Business?

YouTube can do so much for your business it's nearly impossible to know where to begin.

You Can Position Yourself As an Expert

You're probably noticing a recurring theme here. And that is, nearly every social network can help you establish yourself as an expert in your field. Fortunately, YouTube is exceptionally favourable in this regard.

Imagine you are a web designer, who utilises your skills for small businesses. You can then offer a range of services to help these businesses improve their web presence. You could create videos, where you show people the ins and outs of web design.

One video could demonstrate how to register and choose a domain name. Another could teach people how to install Wordpress. This can include an additional video, where you're taking viewers through essential Wordpress plugins.

There is almost no limit to the amount of niche-related videos you could produce around this subject. By doing this, you are demonstrating that you're an authority on web design. It leaves your viewers having no doubt you are indeed an expert. Moreover, it gives your audience the impression you are friendly, helpful and approachable.
At the end of each video, you include a link to your website where people can obtain more information about your services. Providing useful information using this method, can also help you garner viewer loyalty.

A totally different example would be, a retailer who specialises in selling affordable fashion. You could create videos giving people fashion tips, and update your customers on the latest and upcoming trends.

It's an Effective Traffic Generator

One of the biggest benefits of YouTube is that it's a fantastic way for driving traffic to your website. People find your video, watch it and (hopefully) think, "I want to find out more about this company." You can include clickable links directly within your videos, in the video's description, and on your channel's page.

Videos Can Have Tremendous Exposure if They Go Viral

The dream of everyone is to produce a video that goes viral. By viral, I mean it gets watched and shared by thousands, or even millions of people globally. We've all seen a video that seems to appear everywhere, and everyone is talking about it, right?

If that video promotes your brand and business, it can have a great impact for years to come. When a video goes viral, it's almost impossible to stop the traffic and the views it gets. Quite often, this snowball effect is even beyond your control.

What Are the Advantages of Using YouTube?

YouTube Is Extremely User-Friendly

Video is a powerful marketing tool. However, the beauty of YouTube is it's very easy to get started. Creating a channel is simple, whilst it also provides you tools to share and embed your videos outside of the main site.

Modern technology has made it extremely easy to create videos. The camera on an iPhone, for example, is capable of producing excellent quality videos. There is readily available software that makes it relatively easy to edit the videos into something more professional. There are many free (and paid) editors to suit everyone's needs. Apple's iMovie is already on your Mac, plus Microsoft offers Windows Movie Maker.

What Are the Disadvantages of Using YouTube?

<u>Useful or Entertaining Videos Can Be Difficult to Make</u>

It's easy to create a video and then upload it to YouTube. However, creating one that's genuinely useful and/or entertaining for your target audience, is somewhat more difficult. A video needs to be one of those two things if it's going to have any significant impact. Furthermore, it is also important for a video to look professional.

Simon Says: "Why not find a freelancer on Fiverr.com who will edit your videos for you?"

<u>Competition on YouTube Is Extremely High</u>

It is said that more than 100 hours of video are uploaded to YouTube every single minute. This is quite an astounding statistic, which is indicative of its popularity. This is clearly discouraging, however, for anyone who wants his or her video/s to get noticed. The sheer number of them worldwide makes it that more challenging to get views.

Simon Says: "Use SEO tactics within your videos to get more views. This means, researching relevant keywords and adding them to your videos, as well as having a detailed video title and description."

Creating 'Viral' Videos Can Be Difficult

Many businesses delve into YouTube marketing, hoping they're going to create the next viral video that's watched by millions globally. Videos certainly *can* go viral, and many do. The reality is, however, it's quite hard to produce one that captures people's imagination and becomes a YouTube phenomenon.

In many ways, a video going viral is more by luck than intention. Numerous large brands have tried to create such videos and have failed, despite having sizable marketing budgets. A better strategy is, to aim for a more realistic and tangible target. If you produce a viral video, then that's fantastic, but it shouldn't be your main goal.

Pinterest

Pinterest is still relatively unknown by much of the general public. However, it is becoming a significant force in the world of social media and has significant and explosive growth since its launch in 2011.

What Is It and How Does It work?

Pinterest is a social bookmarking website founded by Ben Silbermann, Paul Sciarra and Evan Sharp. The site allows users to discover images of people, places and things in which they're interested. People will then *pin* those items to what are called *boards*. Boards are arranged according to specific subjects of virtually any topic and genre. For example, you might create a board about travel and another about writing a book.

Boards are useful with helping people collect information they need for specific projects. Let's say you were writing a book on the subject, "How to play better tennis." You could create a *tennis* board and pin all the information you find on the internet about that sport.

Pinterest has many similarities to other social networks. Each user has their own profile, which collects their created boards, and all of the items they have pinned. In addition, users can *follow* other members and their boards, as well as like, comment and share posts. This occurs exactly in the same manner as other social networks such as Facebook, Twitter and Google+.

Who Uses Pinterest?

A 2013 study found Pinterest has 70 million users- the majority (80%) of them being female. Over 20 million of these people pinned, re-pinned, or liked a pin during the month of June 2013. Although 71% of users are based in the US, the site has an increasing appeal to people in other regions of the world. Furthermore, only 55% of new registrations occurred in the US during the same month.

Perhaps the figure that immediately jumps out is the 80% female user base. Another 2014 RJ Metrics study also found females are much more engaged with the platform, with 92% of all pins being made by this demographic. The Food & Drink, DIY & Crafts, and Home Décor, are the three most popular pinned subjects. The Food & Drink category alone, makes up 20% of pins.

What Can Pinterest Do for My Business?

One of the main components that make Pinterest interesting to businesses is, pins are often connected with aspirations and action. For example, users pin products they aspire to own. They pin destinations they want to travel to, and they pin recipes they want to try out in the kitchen.

Pinterest Can Help You Build Your Brand

Perhaps one of the most obvious points is, Pinterest can help you build your brand and gain exposure. You can use pins and boards to show off your products and services. You can truly give people an insight into what your business is about, and bring it to life. Moreover, pinning useful content to your boards helps establish your business as an authority in its industry.

It Can Help You Drive Sales

One of the main reasons people use Pinterest is to seek out products they may want to purchase. As a result, Pinterest is a wonderfully effective tool to help retailers drive sales.

It Provides Increased Online Visibility

Pinterest has a vast number of active users. However each time you pin content, it's not only members of the site who will see it. People's boards appear in search results, and it can even help you increase your website's ranking within the search engines. This is the result of the powerful backlinks that come from your Pinterest boards.

What Are the Advantages of Using Pinterest?

Most People Are Buyers

A report by Bizrate indicates 69% of online consumers who use Pinterest, found an item they have purchased (or have wanted to purchase). This is compared to 40% of online buyers who visit Facebook. The survey suggests that significantly more people feel Pinterest is a place 'to get inspiration on what to buy.'

What's more, 43% of users claim they use it, "To associate with retailers or brands with which I identify." 39% said that they use the site, "To get special offers from retailers or brands that I've pinned and/or followed."

It Has an Engaged and Active Community

Recent research found 84% of female users regularly use Pinterest, even after four years from initially registering. Plus, the number of their pins increases each year they use the platform.

On average, a female member makes 42 pins during the first year and increases to approximately 152 pins by year four. This reveals heightened engagement over time, as users integrate Pinterest with more of their online activities. The figures for males are somewhat different, however, with declining numbers after the second year of using the site.

Eye-Catching Visual Imagery is Beneficial for Brands

One of the key advantages of Pinterest is, there's a major focus on visual imagery and its appeal. This is ideal for brands that want to catch their audience's attention, that is, who have attractive products to display. For example, fashion, home and gift retailers, travel businesses, interior designers, etc.

Pinterest's Renown Simplicity

Another prime strength is, the site's features and functions are very user-friendly. In addition, it doesn't try to do everything- it does one thing and does it well. Finally, it also has many similarities with other aforementioned social networks. So even people who haven't used Pinterest previously should find the learning curve relatively small.

It's Easy to Manage

This platform requires relatively little interaction, so there is less pressure to spend time replying to comments or otherwise.

What Are the Disadvantages of Using Pinterest?

The Majority of Users Are Female

While that's great if your business is targeting a female audience, it's not so good if you are trying to appeal to the male market.

It's Not Ideal for All Companies

Indeed, it can be an influential tool for businesses to use images to promote themselves. However many companies feel, they don't have anything valuable to share, nor that their audience uses the platform.

Perhaps a fashion retailer could create boards to present their latest designs, knowing their viewers are primary users of Pinterest. On the contrary, the same probably can't be said for a logistics company.

Summary Points

- Facebook, Twitter, Google+, Linkedin, YouTube, and Pinterest, are currently the main social media networks, however, this could change in the future.

- Social Media sites have some common similarities, however, each platform has a different focus and audience.

- It is essential to know which social media networks your audience uses, so you can focus your attention accordingly.

- Each social media site has its advantages and disadvantages, and it's important to bear these in mind as you use each one.

6. Putting Together Your Social Media Marketing Strategy

You should now be clear on exactly why you should be using social media for your business. You've learned about the various platforms, the way in which they function, and the myriad of advantages, disadvantages and opportunities. It's now time to start looking at how you and your business can start using social media to achieve *results*.

Social Media Marketing Strategy

Before diving in, it is extremely important to know what you are going to do, why you are doing it, and what results you hope to achieve. It is very easy to throw up a Facebook page, register for a Twitter account and then start making posts.

However, doing it in this fashion is unlikely to get you very far on its own. Before getting stuck, it is absolutely imperative to devise a realistic plan. That means, putting together a solid marketing strategy.

Simon Says: "You've probably heard the expression, 'If you fail to plan, you plan to fail.' When it comes to social media, that definitely is true."

You might imagine putting together a marketing strategy is a complicated process. However, this is far from the truth. There are certainly many things you need to consider with any campaign, but your strategy should always aim to be clear and concise. Remember, you are not thinking about this to impress anyone else. You're doing it to be certain so it's unambiguous, since it's for your benefit and that of your audience.

It's also worth noting that over time, you will most likely alter your social media strategy. This will be according to the more you learn about the platforms, what works, and what doesn't work in your industry.

What You should also bear in mind social media is a constantly changing medium. What works well today, may not be the case (or even at all) next year, or even next month. It is imperative to constantly monitor your results and gauge reactions. This is so you can continue to tweak and adapt your campaigns over time.

10 Steps to Ensure a Successful Social Media Marketing Campaign

In this book, we're all about making social media as simple as possible. This is why we have broken this down into ten simple steps to ensure a successful marketing campaign.

1.   Know Your Audience

Before you can be effective with social media, you need to know exactly who your audience is. What gender are they? How old are they? Where do they live? What do they do for a living? What are their likes and dislikes? What are their hobbies? How do they like to spend their time? Are they busy, or do they have lots of free time? Are they affluent, or are they bargain hunters? What purchases have they recently made? Do they donate to charities? If so, which charities?

In terms of social media and internet usage, how much time do they spend online? Which social media websites do they visit each day? How do they access their accounts- through their Smartphone, tablet or laptop? What operating system/s do they use?

The more you know about your audience, the more effectively you'll be able to use this medium to reach out to them specifically. You can directly target the content and style of your posts, to what appeals to your audience the most.

For example, Facebook allows you to target your advertising campaigns to very specific groups (as we talked about earlier). If your audience lives in New York, for example, you can use Facebook's targeting options to focus specifically on people who live there.

How Do You Find Out About Your Audience?

As we have already mentioned, it is imperative to know as much about your audience as possible. Although you should have already acquired a good amount of information about them, there are always more details to be uncovered.

Market Research

Conducting basic market research helps you find out a great deal about your viewership. A simple survey sent out to your existing customers could uncover an abundance of information that you might not have otherwise known. Remember, market research is not just about figures and numbers (quantitative research).

Qualitative research, which is where you discover information about people's feelings, views, perspectives, concerns, etc., can be invaluable. This will pay off in spades with helping you succeed in marketing.

Website Analytics

A tool such as Google Analytics can be installed onto your website. It will allow you to track exactly who visits your site and when they visit. It provides extremely useful data about your visitors, their demographic profile and interests, geographic location, behaviour, and technology choices. By analysing who comes to your website and their characteristics, you should be able to identify various trends. This can help you more clearly focus your campaigns accordingly.

Looking at Existing Buyer Data

You probably already have a great deal of information about your existing customers. So don't forget to use it to its full potential. As well as guiding your social media activities, the data you already possess can help you shape the market research in which you conduct.

Different Audiences

It is also important to remember, you might want to reach several different audiences through your social media activities. Potential groups that can be acquired through social media might include:

- Prospective new customers
- Current customers
- Lapsed customers
- Associates of the end user
- Potential joint venture partners
- Suppliers
- Journalists and bloggers

Whomever you're trying to target and the more you know about your audience, the easier it will be to plan a campaign that gets you the desired results.

2. Understand Who Is Your Ideal Client or Customer

No two clients or customers are going to be the same. Therefore, it is important to have a clear picture of who is your ideal customer. This is so you can craft social media campaigns that *speak directly to them*. If you could choose any buyer for your product or service, who would they be?

Create a Pen Portrait

One of the easiest ways of getting clear about your model customer is, create a pen portrait. This is where you write down a description of the person you have in mind as your *perfect buyer*. This portrait includes specific details about their background, current situation, lifestyle, etc.

Here's an example:

> *John Smith is aged 29 and has a partner called Sarah. They live in a contemporary apartment in the trendy area of Wimbledon, South West London. John has a degree in*

marketing. He currently works as a marketing manager for a technology company, where he oversees a team of five people.

John likes to work hard and play harder. He always seems to be in a rush, however, he prefers it that way and enjoys the pace of the London lifestyle. He regularly works 11-hour days. However, he enjoys his work and believes that his strong work ethic is the reason why he has been successful in his career.

John is concerned about his appearance to others. So he likes to dress well and enjoys wearing designer brands- particularly Ted Baker. He also drives a BMW and likes to keep up with technology. Therefore having the latest iPhone model is an absolute must. John and Sarah enjoy their food and like to dine out at restaurants at least twice a week. They are very proud of their home, and also like to host dinner parties with friends and family . . . etc.

Points to Cover

You could continue this example and delve into all aspects of their life. The more specific and detailed you get, the better you'll be able to target your campaigns accordingly.

- What is his or her name?
- How old are they?
- What is their background?
- Where do they live?
- Where do they work?
- How educated are they?
- What position are they in currently?
- Are they happy with this position?
- Who do they aspire to be?
- What do they like?
- What do they dislike?
- How do they like to spend their time?
- Who is their peer group?
- How do they dress?
- How much time do they have?
- What are their pains?

Why Is Customer Analysis So Important?

If you know who you are talking to, it makes everything you do on social media so much easier. Every time you take an action such as making a comment, posting a status update, or sharing a video, you should have your ideal customer in mind. By doing this, it's possible to more easily craft campaigns that speak directly to your audience.

In the example above, we said John lives a fast-paced lifestyle and always seems to be in a rush. If this is your ideal customer, then you know that posting 2,000-word tutorials to your Facebook page might not be the most effective strategy. Such people simply won't have the time to read it. If your audience is short on time, then it makes sense to concentrate on succinct but useful messages.

If you know the person's likes and dislikes, then you can appeal to these things in your comments. The same applies to their pains. If we looked at a different example, and you knew your ideal customer hates their job, then you can discuss this in your messages. Tapping into the beliefs, likes, dislikes, and pain points, can be extremely powerful in marketing. This will result with you truly resonating with your specific audience. It will make them sit up and think, "This company is talking to ME."

It is possible you may create multiple pen portraits, to cater to different types of people who make up your audience. However, you shouldn't have too many variations. Otherwise, you will end up trying to talk to everyone, and will resonate with nobody.

3. Understand What You Are Trying to Achieve

Quite honestly, you cannot move forward with anything if you don't know what you're striving for. Therefore, it is very important to set clear goals at the earliest opportunity. You need to understand and decide what specifically you want to achieve from your social media activities. This is so you can start working towards those goals in a strategic, comprehensive manner.

Here are some examples:

- Use social media to increase sales
- Use social media to increase market share
- Use social media to increase brand awareness

The goals you set will determine the rest of your social media strategy. If one of your objectives, for example, is to increase sales, then you can work towards putting together a strategy to make this happen.

4. Write Down Your Marketing Objectives

Once you have established your goals, you should then break these down into specific marketing objectives.

Marketing objectives are imperative with helping you plan your social media campaigns. Everything you do on these sites will be geared towards assisting you to achieve these goals.

Marketing objectives should be specific, measurable, achievable, realistic, and time-specific (SMART).

Specific - It is important that you are as specific as possible, so you know exactly what you are aiming for.

Measurable - By making your objectives measurable, you will be able to know precisely what you set out to achieve and the time frame involved.

Achievable - It is no use formulating objectives that aren't achievable. For example, having an objective to *generate 1,000 new leads in the next 24 hours,* probably wouldn't be attainable.

Realistic - It is also important that objectives are realistic within the operations of the company. Does the business have the skills, means, and time to achieve the goal that has been set?

Time Specific - You need to know *when* you expect to reach your target goal. Outline a time frame that is attainable and manageable, when also taking into account the other obligations of the business.

If one of your goals is to *increase sales,* then one of your objectives might be:

"In the next 30 days, we will generate 50 new leads to our website via Facebook advertising, and convert at least 5 of those leads into sales."

5. Spy on the Competition

You need to spy on the competition to be aware of how they use social media.

You can learn a lot about how to effectively use social media, just by looking at how your competitors are utilising it.

I'm not suggesting you should go out and copy the specific strategies of your competitors (it's important to be distinctive and unique). However, you can certainly do some research and see what is working (and what isn't) within your industry.
One of the beauties of social media is its apparent transparency. A post on any network that creates a lot of buzz, will be immediately obvious, due to its high number of comments, likes, re-tweets, shares, etc.

By studying businesses that are already successful, you can get new ideas for your company. As I say, it is very important to stand out and try to be exclusive and notable. However, at the same time, there is often little point in completely re-inventing the wheel.

6. Pick Social Media Sites That Best Suit Your Business and Prioritise Your Action Plan Accordingly

It is essential to assess which social platforms can best help you achieve your goals and objectives. Perhaps one of your primary goals is, to network with other businesses in your industry, and seek out possible joint ventures. Linkedin would be the ideal place to do this.

If you want to use social media to find new customers or clients directly, then Facebook could provide that perfect platform. Establishing yourself as an expert and authority may be best achieved through a mixture of Facebook, Twitter, Google+ and YouTube.

It is also important to find out where your target audience hangs out. If they don't use a particular social network, then you might decide not to use it, at least for the time being.

Once you've discovered which networks can help you meet your goals and your audience's chosen platform, you can prioritise which sites to put forth your efforts. With so many different social networks in existence (and more than we've had time to cover in this book), it's often impractical to spread your marketing efforts too thinly.

Simon Says: "It is much better to concentrate on two or three social networks and utilise them well rather than trying to master all of them, and waste vast amounts of time with networks that aren't ideally suited to your business."

Of course, situations change over time. Therefore you may decide to join more networks in the future as your business grows, and/or the world of social media changes.

7. Create Content in Blocks and Schedule the Posts in Advance to Help Automate the Process

Before you actively get started with social media, you need to think about how to create content of value. It is one thing to set up a Facebook profile—that's the easy part. The challenging element is, posting pertinent, meaningful information. This means posting useful and valuable content to create audience engagement.

112

What's more, this content needs to be posted on your social platforms on a regular basis. It is no use making one Facebook post a month because people are going to forget about your business.

I'll be honest with you. Creating and posting substantial content on a regular basis, is a challenge for many businesses. You only have to look at the number of neglected social profiles, to know this is true. However, by doing a little planning and working *smarter,* it doesn't have to be a huge challenge!

Let's take a more in-depth look at content . . .

Coming Up with Content Ideas

Many businesses struggle with knowing exactly what to post to their social media accounts. However, it is vital that you get this right because posting worthwhile content is at the heart of using social media successfully.

If you're stuck for content ideas, then you will need to do some research and brainstorm potential concepts.

Social Media itself is a valuable place to do this because it allows you to find out what your target audience is talking about. Try to spend some time every week looking at social media pages that are related to your business/industry/niche, etc.

What questions are people asking? What arc thc main topics of conversation? Linkedin can be particularly beneficial for this. However, other platforms can also provide you with invaluable insights.

You can apply this outside of these platforms, by looking at online forums and discussions groups. Again, have a read through threads and find out what people are discussing.

In addition, have a look at some of your competitors and observe the type of content they post to their accounts. As mentioned before, the idea isn't to copy exactly what they are doing. However, there is absolutely nothing wrong with taking concepts and putting your spin on them. Few methodologies in the universe are ever 100% original.

Also, don't forget to listen to your audience outside of the online world. Keep your ears to the ground at all times. Keep track of content ideas that can come to you at any time. They can often occur in the most unlikely of places. You may overhear a conversation whilst having lunch in a cafe, for example, and it triggers a great idea for an engaging piece of content.

Simon Says: "Use software to schedule your posts in advance and help automate the process.

Create a Content Calendar

When planning out content to be posted to your social media accounts, it can be extremely useful to create a content calendar. This is a simple plan of what you are going to post—and when you are going to post it.

You can download an example of a content calendar and a FREE template at **www.simplesimonspublishing.com/resources**

Create Content in Advance, Then Schedule It to Be Posted Automatically

As previously mentioned, it is necessary to add content to your social media accounts on a regular basis. If you want to engage your audience, you simply cannot have weeks and weeks pass between posts.

An effective system in this area is, to bulk-create your content in advance, then schedule it to be posted automatically over time. By doing this, it makes it much easier to stay on top of things and greatly reduces the administrative burden.

Firstly, you can spend an hour or two planning your content for the following week. Then you can use a tool such as Hootsuite for scheduling, where it's posted automatically over that week. This is rather than having to remember to log in several times each day to manually post. In addition, such tools allow you to manage all of your accounts from one place. This is easier than logging in separately to Facebook, Twitter, Google+, etc.

How Often Should Businesses Post to Social Media?

In all honesty, there isn't a solid answer to that question. However, you should try to post regularly if you want to keep yourself in people's minds.

Furthermore, it's better to work on only two or three sites and add content several times a week. This is rather than having six different social media pages and only update them weekly.

8. Allow a Reasonable Budget to Get You Started

A crucial element of your marketing strategy is your budget. This should form part of your overall strategic marketing blueprint.

Many businesses start out by establishing a budget and then work out what goals they can achieve within that budget. However, it's usually better to do it the other way around and begin by assembling what you want to achieve initially. Social Media shouldn't be seen as an expense—it should be considered an investment in your business. If it is implemented correctly, then it should provide a sizable return on that investment.

A big mistake many businesses make is to allocate a very low budget to their marketing activities. However, it is necessary to allow a reasonable budget to get you started. It is certainly true you can run successful campaigns with relatively little investment. But you'll need to invest some money into your campaigns in order to kick-start them.

Having said that, it is also important to not just throw a load of money into Facebook advertising, for example. Subsequently, you may think this will enable you to see immediate success and results. It is vital to set your objectives first, and then work out a realistic budget that will enable you to achieve your goals.
In addition, you will probably want to focus on certain components of your budget, depending on how quickly it can provide you with an ROI. As an example, you might decide to prioritise spending money on Facebook advertising. This is something that can quickly bring in revenue (e.g. Facebook adverts that point to your online store). Other goals and objectives, such as achieving long-term engagement, may come lower down your priority list when you first get started.

9. Track Your Results Closely and Respond if Necessary

One of the most important aspects to consider when using social media is, it's essential to closely monitor responses to your campaigns. You then need to optimise/tweak your campaigns accordingly for maximum results.

Remember social media is not just about making posts and sharing content. It's about achieving results to help you grow your business and ultimately acquire more profit. There is absolutely no point in posting every day for an entire year if it doesn't generate your desired results/goals.

10. Make it part of your Ongoing Marketing Strategy

Social media is not something that you do once and stop. It has to become part of your ongoing marketing strategy. Social media can have a massive impact on your business and can be relatively inexpensive to implement.

Adding regular updates and news is not a difficult or even that time consuming once you get started. As we have already covered, you can schedule your updates and posts which means that you can create your content in advance and post it over a week or a month.

How Do You Track Your Results?

The good news is, there are many different tools which can help you track your campaign results.

Facebook, for example, provides detailed statistics about your Facebook page. This includes General Page Metrics, Page Post Metrics, and details of *Likes*, reach and engagement.

For each post on your page you can see:

- The number of people your post reached
- The number of people who clicked your post
- The number of people who liked, commented on, or shared your post

You can also see audience demographic information as well. These data shows viewers who like your page, the number of page views, figures on how people are finding your page, etc.

Additionally, you can integrate your Facebook advertising campaigns with your Google Analytics account. This allows you to measure the impact your Facebook ads have on your business. You can even track how many people click on your adverts, and how many of those people visit your website or take an action.

Social Media is Constantly Changing

Here's something else to consider. Just because something works well this week, it doesn't necessarily mean that it will work well next week. The world of social media is constantly changing, and so are consumer attitudes, wants, needs, and desires.

Summary Points

- It is essential to put together a marketing strategy, so you know what you want to achieve and how you are going to achieve it.

- The more you know about your audience, the better. When you truly understand to whom you are speaking, you can create extremely powerful marketing messages that attract and engage your target audience.

- It is important to post on a regular basis and to provide valuable, compelling content. Consider putting together a content calendar, and then use social media software to automate the process.

- Allow a reasonable budget to get started with social media marketing.

- You will need to monitor results closely, and constantly tweak/optimise your campaigns in order to achieve the best possible outcome.

7. Getting Involved

One area where many businesses struggle is how to best implement their marketing strategy. Is it better to do it all in-house? Or, would it be better to outsource it all to social media experts?

There are of course advantages and disadvantages to both methods. The way in which you choose will very much depend on the scale of what you are trying to achieve. This also includes your budget, and other resources available in your business.

Many companies choose to use a hybrid strategy. This is where they conduct some tasks in-house, and outsource those that are beyond the scope of their expertise or skill set.

Outsourcing Social Media Management

Several businesses will feel like they need assistance with their social media activities. Even if you're confident and have the time and resources to manage it in-house, it's often worthwhile to outsource tasks.

Outsourcing can reduce in-house pressures, and tap into the knowledge/skills of experts. External social media specialists can help you examine aspects you might not have otherwise considered. They can also help improve the rate at which you see success from your campaigns.

Web Marketing Agencies

There are many full-service online marketing agencies that can help you develop an impactful strategy for your business. In addition, they can assist with implementing and managing your social media campaigns on a day-to-day basis.

The downside to using a marketing agency is, of course, the price. Fees can be expensive, and they often charge by the hour. This can mean you need to make significant expenditures even before obtaining any results from your efforts.

Despite this, hiring a marketing agency can also be worthwhile. It's advantageous if you want to avoid the day-to-day worries of managing your campaigns. Initially, it may appear cheaper to manage it all yourself. However, you also have to consider whether managing everything in-house, is the best use of your time and resources.

Freelancers/Consultants

It may be possible you need help with specific aspects of your social media activities, but you don't need a full-service marketing agency. You then might want to consider hiring individual freelancers or consultants. You can hire them on a long-term basis (using a freelance virtual assistant). Or, you can hire a freelancer for a one-off project (hiring an individual to design you an eye-catching banner for your Facebook page).

Taking this approach is obviously cheaper. Moreover, it still allows you access to specialist skills and expertise you might not necessarily have in-house. Furthermore, the advantage of this approach is that it is flexible. You can gain access to these skills whenever you need them.

In-House Social Media Management

Many businesses will have a dedicated social media manager. This may also include an in-house team to help implement and manage relevant activities. The advantage is, it makes certain tasks easier, while enabling you to tap into the specialist expertise of the industry. Although you certainly could outsource an article that explains specific issues within the market but producing this content in-house may result in better content.

Hybrid Strategy

Various companies will choose to have an in-house marketing manager or team. At the same time, they will also outsource certain elements of their social media activities.

Even if you feel you have sufficient in-house skills and expertise, it's important to utilise these in an efficient way. This is why it is often sensible to take a hybrid approach. Trying to manage everything in-house often isn't the best use of time and resources.

Is it practical to use your marketing manager's time updating Twitter, tagging posts, and adding keywords? A better alternative may be to outsource those duties, while your in-house team concentrates on the overall strategy of the business. Social Media admin tasks can be outsourced to a virtual assistant.

Summary Points

- It is important to decide exactly how you are going to manage your social media activities. You will need to know which aspects you are going to outsource, and which things you want to manage in-house.

- Outsourcing social media management, allows you to take advantage of specialist marketing expertise while freeing up in-house resources.

- Certain tasks are often better handled in-house, such as those that require specific industry-related proficiency.

- Many businesses choose to take a hybrid approach. They will manage certain components in-house while outsourcing specialised tasks that extend beyond the company's parameters— which would be more cost-effective to outsource as a whole.

8. 'Need-to-Know' Social Media Terminology

One of the things that people tend to find confusing about social media is, there is a lot of terminology involved. If you don't know your hashtags from your micro-blogging, then you should find the following A-Z list of 'need-to-know' terminology extremely useful.

@
Seen within social media posts. The @ symbol is used to tag a particular user in a post. Placing @JoeBloggs at the end of a Tweet, for example, would tag the Twitter user "JoeBloggs" within the Tweet.

App
Short for *application*. A social media app is a piece of software that runs on a smartphone or tablet. It enables people to browse a particular social media platform.

Blog
An online publishing platform where an author posts articles regularly. The newest article usually appears at the top of the blog.

Campaign
A word used to describe the collective elements of a marketing campaign. A social media marketing campaign, for example, might include using Facebook, Twitter and YouTube.

Cloud Computing
The practice of storing files and data on remote servers hosted on the internet. Documents stored in the cloud can easily be edited and shared with anyone who has an internet connection.

Comments
Voicing an opinion on posts made on social media sites. Comments normally appear below the post that was made by the original author.

Crowdfunding
The practice of funding projects by raising small amounts of money from a number of different people.

Crowdsourcing
The practice of obtaining information or services from different people, who come together to make a project a reality.

eBook
An electronic book that is viewed through an e-reader (e.g. Kindle device) or another electronic device, such as a computer, smartphone or tablet.

Embedding
Placing a video, image or other digital file that is located on one website (e.g. YouTube) then inserting it on another platform (e.g. your website).

Facebook
A popular social networking website.

Follow
To 'Follow' someone on social media means opting-in to receive their social media updates.

Friend
A contact on Facebook.

Google+
A popular social networking website.

Hashtag
A way of tagging a social media post with a certain subject. Users can click on a #hashtag and see other social media users who are posting about the same subject.

Hosted Accounts
When you set up an account on Facebook or one of the other networks, you do so on their servers. This is known as a hosted account.

Influencer
An authoritative social media user, who has the ability to influence the actions of other social media users.

Keyword
A term used in Search Engine Optimisation (SEO). A keyword is a word or phrase within web content. It's designed to make the text appear in the search engine results when a user searches for that keyword.

Like
A social media feature that allows people to express their approval of a post by clicking a *Like* button. A social media post that has a high number of 'Likes', signals to other users that the content has a high level of importance and is useful, funny, informative, poignant, etc.

LinkedIn
A popular social networking website for business professionals.

Metadata
Data that is collected about the user, device, and activities taking place.

Metatags
Used in HTML web pages to provide information about the page.

Microblog
A social media platform where users provide short, frequent updates. An example of a micro-blogging platform is Twitter.

MySpace
A social networking website that now focuses on musicians. MySpace was at one time the most popular networking website, however, it was overtaken by Facebook.

Newsfeed
The newsfeed is a feature of popular social media platforms like Facebook. It brings together posts made by other users with whom the initial person is connected.

Permalink
A permanent URL that points to a specific web page or other piece of online content.

Pinterest
A popular social bookmarking website that focuses on images.

Platform
Another term for a social network. Facebook, Twitter, Google+, etc. are all social media platforms.

Podcast
An audio file that is made available to download or stream from the internet. It's typically created in the format of a series. Each podcast is usually dedicated to a specific subject, with users being able to subscribe to receive new episodes.

Post
A post is an article, comment, image, or link that is *posted* to a website.

PPC

Pay Per Click (PPC) is an advertising solution offered by networks such as Google and Bing. Advertisers pay 'X' amount of money each time a user clicks on their advert. An example of PPC would be Google AdWords.

Profile

A page on a social networking website which shows more information about the user.

RSS

Rich Site Summary (RSS) is a web format used to publish frequently updated web content, such as news, blog posts, video and audio.

Self-Hosted

Self-hosted is where you install and run software scripts or programs, on your own or a 3rd party server or hosting account.

SEO

Search Engine Optimisation (SEO) is the process of optimising a website, with the aim of improving the position of the website within search results.

Social Bookmarking

A Social Media platform that allows users to make and share bookmarks of web documents with others.

Social Media

A term used to describe sites that allow users to create and share content. Examples of social media platforms include Facebook, Twitter, and Google+.

Status Update

A social media post in which the user shares what they are currently doing or any content he or she feels is newsworthy.

Tags
A label added to a social media post that provides information about the subject of said post.

Trackback
A notification that is sent automatically when someone links to an online document (for example a blog post).

Tweet
A post made on the Twitter social networking platform.

Twitter
A popular social networking website.

Viral
It comes from the terminology to *spread like a virus*. It's a technique that uses social media to get a message *shared* to the masses rapidly. Gangnam Style is an example of a video that went viral on a global scale drawing massive media attention.

Vlog
A term used to describe a video blog.

Wall
A page that displays all social media posts and interactions made by a user.

Web 2.0
A term used to describe the second stage development of the internet. The first stage of the Internet revolved around static web pages. Web 2.0 is characterised by dynamic, user-generated content (e.g. social media).

Webinar
A seminar that is conducted over the internet.

White Paper
An electronic or printed document that briefs the reader on a particular subject.

Wordpress
A very well-known Content Management System (CMS). Wordpress can be installed on web space, and allows the user to create a blog or website. A Wordpress website can be customised with themes and plugins which alter the look and features of its pages.

YouTube
A popular video sharing website.

9. Additional Tools and Resources

Tools

There are a number of tools available which can help you in various aspects of your marketing. Tools which would be beneficial in areas such as: following trends and brands, finding articles and news relevant to your business, preparing, scheduling, publishing and tracking your campaigns in all of your accounts.

More information can be found at
http://www.simplesimonspublishing.com/resources

Buddypress - WordPress Plugin
Buddypress is a plugin that turns WordPress into a social media website.

Dlv.it
A multi-channel and multi-faceted distribution service.

Elgg.org & Friendica
Elgg and Friendica are self-hosted tools that allow you to create your own custom social networking sites. They can be installed on the same server and domain as your company website. You have full control over privacy, and you set the rules.

Hootsuite
Hootsuite Pro lets small and medium-sized businesses and agencies manage their social media presence across more than 35 social networks.

IFTT
Stands for- *If This, Then That*. They are scripts known as *recipes* to automate repetitive tasks. This is based on the notion that if 'this' happens, then 'that' will happen. For example, you can set it up so that, "If I'm tagged in a photo on Facebook... then send me a text message."

Ning
Ning is a hosted system that allows you to create your own custom social networks and enables you to have full control of your community.

Postplanner - Facebook
This tool will help you run your Facebook campaigns more efficiently. It includes a number of useful features that permits you to find and then share what is popular in your niche.

Sprout Social
Works across all social media networks and helps manage and track your campaigns.

SocialOomph
Primarily to help you automate your social media accounts on Facebook, Twitter and Linkedin. It also works with RSS feeds, Plurk and blogs.

Zapier
Similar to IFTT, Zapier provides event-based automation to help you with following your social media campaigns.

Other Social Media Websites

We have covered many of the most popular and widely used social media platforms thus far. However, incorporating the several other networks available in great detail would have exceeded the scope of this book.

The social platforms below are by no means an extensive list. These are additional websites of which you should be aware. Therefore, investigate further to see if their systems and features would coincide with your business.

It is always worth remembering that the world of social media is constantly changing. There will be new sites and platforms cropping up all the time. It is important to keep track of the latest trends and shifts with various sites that people are using. This is so you don't miss out on potential opportunities in the future.

Flickr
Flickr is a photo management platform that allows users to upload, and then share their photographs and videos with other Flickr members.

Reddit
Reddit is a social media news site, which allows the user to share content such as links or text posts. Users then vote content *up* or *down*.

Snapchat
An instant photo-messaging based site that permits users to send photos and videos to fellow contacts. Its unique twist is, the content is only shown to the recipient between one and ten seconds. This however, depends on the chosen settings of the respective user/s. After this time has elapsed, the *snap* is then deleted.

StumbleUpon

A social media platform that finds and then recommends web content. It allows users to discover a myriad of things in which they're interested.

Tumblr

Tumblr is a micro-blogging platform. It allows members to post content to their own micro-blog and follow the blogs created by other users.

Vine

Vine is a video-based platform where users create and share short looping videos.

Conclusion

Hopefully, you will have now have a firmer handle on social media, and will be able to make use of the information in this book.

Remember that this expansive and powerful medium is constantly changing. There could well be some truly useful sites, both now and in the future, that will surely be beneficial to your specific industry.

You can contact us at info@simplesimonspublishing.com with any comments, questions or feedback.

Did you enjoy this book?

You can find more useful resources at **www.simplesimonspublishing.com/resources**

I want to thank you sincerely for purchasing and reading this book. I hope you got a lot out of it to help build and maximise your marketing strategies.

Can I ask a quick favour of you?

If you enjoyed this book, I would appreciate it if you could please leave me an honest review on Amazon.

I love getting feedback from my customers, and reviews on Amazon do make a difference. I read all my reviews and would appreciate your thoughts.

Thanks so much!

Simple Simon

Don't forget your FREE gift which can be found at

www.simplesimonspublishing.com/freegift

ALL RIGHTS RESERVED.

Written by Lloyd Hester

www.lloydhester.com

www.ingramcontent.com/pod-product-compliance
Lightning Source LLC
Chambersburg PA
CBHW020918180526
45163CB00007B/2795